The Egg Thieves

Joan Lingard

Illustrations by Paul Howard

Catnip

CATNIP BOOKS
Published by Catnip Publishing Ltd
Quality Court, off Chancery Lane
London WC2A 1HR

This edition first published 2014
1 3 5 7 9 10 8 6 4 2

First published in Great Britain in 1999 by Hodder Children's Books.

Text copyright © Joan Lingard, 1999
Ilustrations copyright © Paul Howard, 1999
The right of Joan Lingard and Paul Howard to be identified as the
Author and Illustrator of the Work has been asserted by them in
accordance with the Copyright, Design and Patents Act 1988.

Cover illustration by Steven Wood
Cover design by Pip Johnson

A CIP catalogue record for this book is available from the British
Library.

ISBN 978-1-84647-179-7

Printed in Poland

www.catnippublishing.co.uk

For Amy and Shona
with love

The Egg Thieves

Chapter One

It was Lecky Grant who saw the egg thieves leaving. Something wakened him early that morning. He slipped out of bed and went to the window. His house was opposite the pine wood where the ospreys had their nest.

It was a misty morning. The trees had that shrouded, ghostly look that made you shiver a little. But the car that was sitting in the path that led into the wood had nothing to do with ghosts. It looked solid. And although the engine was running softly, Lecky could hear it clearly.

He ran through to his parents' bedroom shouting, 'Dad, egg thieves!'

He didn't wait for an answer but tore down the stairs in his bare feet and pyjamas. He yanked open the front door. The car was manoeuvring out on to the road.

'Stop!' Lecky dashed out in front of it waving his arms.

His father, coming up behind him, shouted, 'Get back, Lecky! Don't be an idiot!'

The car swerved round Lecky, its tyres screeching on the loose gravel at the side of the road. For a moment it looked as if it might mount the bank. Then it righted itself and, picking up speed, raced off.

'Never do that again!' said Mr Grant. 'You could have been killed.'

Now Mrs Grant appeared on the doorstep, pulling on her dressing gown. 'Come inside at once, Lecky!' she commanded. 'Look at you – out there in your pyjamas! *And* bare feet! You'll catch your death of cold. You, too,' she added to her husband.

She filled the kettle while her husband phoned the police station. PC Murray said he'd be right along. He was the only police officer in the village.

'Bit late now, though, isn't it?' said Mrs Grant. 'Trying to lock the stable door when the horse has gone.'

'They might have left clues,' said Lecky hopefully. 'Footprints. Things like that. We should go and look, Dad.'

'Away and get yourself dressed first!' said his mother. 'I'm not wanting you going out into the wood half naked.'

Lecky dressed quickly. He had just finished when PC Murray arrived. The constable looked as if he hadn't had time to comb his hair.

Mrs Grant set a pot of tea on the table, and a pile of warm, buttered toast.

'Sit in,' she said. 'It's a chilly morning. Better to go out with something in your stomach.'

'It would have been egg thieves, I

suppose?' said the constable, warming his hands round a mug of tea.

'I'm afraid so,' said Mr Grant glumly. 'Who else would be parking there this early in the morning?'

'*And* they took off without lights,' said Lecky. 'So they must have been up to something.'

PC Murray sighed and brought out his notebook and ballpoint pen. 'Can you give me a description of the car?'

'Saloon,' said Mr Grant. 'Two-door.'

'Don't suppose either of you got the car number?'

'There was mud over the number plate,' said Lecky.

'Aye, there would be! Camouflage. Colour?'

'Dark,' said Lecky.

The constable wrote that down. 'No idea what colour of dark?'

'Navy blue. Maybe black. I'm not sure, are you, Dad? It all happened so quickly and it wasn't quite light.'

'That's when they come, these hooligans!' said the constable.

But they knew it was unlikely that they would have been hooligans out just to vandalise the nest. They'd have been proper egg thieves who would sell the eggs to collectors. Osprey eggs were rare and in demand. At one time the birds had been wiped out altogether in Britain.

'They'll be miles away by now,' said Mr Grant. It was known that people would drive hundreds of miles to raid nests.

Some osprey nests were kept under constant watch by the Royal Society for the Protection of Birds. Their nest wasn't one of those. Lecky complained about that now.

'It's not fair!'

'The RSPB can't protect every single nest in the country,' said his father.

The local people tried to keep a watchful eye themselves on the ospreys. They thought of them as 'their' ospreys. The nest was meant to be a secret, but how could it be a real secret when everybody round about knew it was there?

'How many in the car?' asked PC Murray.

'Two,' said Lecky. 'Both in the front.'

'Male?'

'I think so.'

'Difficult to be absolutely certain,' said Mr Grant.

The constable nodded, closed his notebook and tucked it into his top pocket.

When they had drunk their tea and eaten the toast, they crossed the road,

Lecky, his dad, and PC Murray. They took a lightweight aluminium ladder with them and Mr Grant carried a long pole which had a mirror attached to its end.

On the track into the wood they saw the tyre marks the car had left in the mud. The thieves would have had no other choice but to park only a mere stone's throw from the road. Two large boulders blocked the rest of the path. They'd been put there to stop motorbikers getting into the wood. Or cars, carrying egg thieves!

'Look,' cried Lecky, 'footprints!'

They bent to examine them. They looked fresh.

'You can't tell anything from that lot,' said PC Murray. 'Just that they were wearing heavy boots.'

'One of them had spikes on their

shoes, though,' Mr Grant pointed out.

PC Murray nodded. 'Good for climbing trees.'

The ospreys' nest was in a clearing, a little way into the wood, at the top of a very tall pine tree. Barbed wire encircled the lower part of the trunk. It was meant to deter thieves but it obviously hadn't.

The parent ospreys were not on the nest. They were sitting on the top of another tree close by, level with the nest, watching it closely. They were big birds, roughly sixty centimetres in length, and

their wing spans, at full stretch, would measure as much as one hundred and fifty centimetres. They were dark brown in colour, with white undersides.

'They've been, that's for sure!' said Mr Grant. 'The thieves. The female would be sitting on the nest if they hadn't.'

The nest was large—it would need to be to house such big birds. Perched right on the top of the tree, constructed mostly from large pieces of stick, it was a raggedy-looking affair. It could easily be seen from the ground below. Last year Lecky and his dad had found an abandoned nest. It had measured a metre across and seventy-five centimetres in depth.

Mr Grant took a closer look at the trunk of the tree just above the barbed wire. 'I can see the mark of his spikes.'

'Will you go up or will I?' asked PC

Murray, who, it was well known, had a poor head for heights. Last year he'd had to rescue a kitten stuck halfway up a rowan tree. He'd felt dizzy before he'd got anywhere near her.

'I'll go,' said Mr Grant. He was a forester and didn't mind climbing tall trees. Neither did Lecky, but he knew his father wouldn't let him do it.

PC Murray propped the ladder against the trunk of the tree and Lecky helped him steady it. Mr Grant, with the pole held firmly in his hand, climbed slowly up. The ospreys didn't like this, not one little bit!

They uttered cries of alarm. They flapped their wings. They rose into the air, showing off their huge wing spans and white undersides. They looked magnificent and terrifying. They made you want to duck and cover your head with your arms. Lecky swallowed. What if they were to attack his dad?

'Sorry to do this to you, guys,' said Mr Grant, squinting up at them.

The birds continued to circle the treetops, flapping their wings and uttering fierce, threatening cries.

Mr Grant raised the long pole until

the mirror was suspended over the nest and he could see inside. Lecky and PC Murray waited anxiously below.

'They've taken the lot!' said Mr Grant.

'Oh no!' cried Lecky.

'I'm afraid so,' said his dad. 'All three eggs are gone.'

Chapter Two

The whole village was furious, once the news spread. The talk that morning was of nothing else in the shop-cum-post office.

'The nerve of them!' said Nora McPhee, whose father was the postmaster. In the mornings, for half an hour before going to school, she helped her mother behind the shop counter. People came in at that time for milk and papers.

'It's no one from the village, anyway,

that's obvious!' said Mrs McPhee.

'How can you tell that?' asked old Mr Taylor, who lived two doors away and had come along in his slippers to fetch his paper.

'Stands to reason, doesn't it? They were in a car. They must be outsiders.'

'Somebody local could have tipped them off.'

'You're right, Mr Taylor,' said Nora, finding that an interesting idea. 'They could!'

'Now who would do a thing like that?' said Mrs McPhee.

'I could think of someone,' said Mr Taylor knowingly.

They knew who he meant. Dod Smith, who lived up the back of the village in an old ramshackle cottage, had taken a brand new spade from Mr Taylor's shed last summer. Mr Taylor hadn't forgiven him even though he'd got it back. PC Murray had gone up to Dod's place and fetched it. Dod had said he'd only borrowed it, but he was known to be a bit 'light-fingered'. He never took anything much, usually a tool or something he needed. And often as not, when he'd finished with it, he'd return it.

'How would Dod know how to contact egg thieves?' demanded Mrs McPhee.

'He knows more than you think!' said Mr Taylor.

'I think that's enough on that subject,' put in Mr McPhee, who was sorting sheets of stamps at the post office counter.

The old man took his newspaper and shuffled out.

Mr McPhee shook his head. 'Too much gossip goes on in this place.'

'Mind you, I do remember seeing Dod

talking to two men in a dark car back in the summer,' said Mrs McPhee. 'It wasn't a car I knew by sight.'

'Well, keep the information to yourself!' said her husband. 'You too, Nora! They might just have been asking the way. We're not wanting to start false rumours.'

The school was also seething with the news of the theft. Lecky told his story several times over and Mrs Fraser, the teacher, asked him to write it up in the school diary.

Mrs Fraser was their only teacher. She lived in a house at the side of the school, along with her husband, who was the local vet, and their two children, Jessie and Johnny, aged six and seven. They were pupils at the school. There were seventeen pupils in all, ranging from Primary One to

Primary Seven. They worked in groups in the same room and the big ones helped the little ones. Their room was bright and cheerful and the walls were covered with stories and drawings and photographs. In pride of place was a large coloured photo of an osprey in flight, its wings stretched wide.

'Today,' wrote Lecky, 'a crime was committed in the wood.'

'A terrible crime,' insisted Nora, who was sitting beside him watching him write. 'Well, it *was* terrible. For the ospreys. And us.'

'Oh, all right.' He added, 'A terrible crime.'

'The criminals must be caught and punished,' said Nora. 'Put that down too!'

'I can put it down,' he scoffed. 'But who's going to catch them? Mr Murray says he's got nothing much to go on. There are too many dark cars on the roads.'

'I might have something to go on,' said Nora mysteriously.

'You!'

'I just could have an idea for a suspect,' she said, dropping her voice.

'Oh yes?' He knew Nora McPhee! She had a great imagination. 'So who do you think it is?'

'Tell you later.'

At breaktime, in the playground, they went over by the back wall. A ewe was feeding her lamb on the other side. The field was dotted with sheep. The noise of their bleating filled the air.

'Cross your heart, Lecky Grant, and promise you won't tell anyone else!' demanded Nora. 'My dad would kill me.'

'Tell them what?'

'Promise!'

'OK, I promise!' Lecky rolled his eyes. He was curious, though, to know who she had in mind. Some batty idea, more than likely.

'My mum saw Dod Smith talking to two men in a dark car last summer.'

'Is that all?' said Lecky. '*Hundreds* of dark cars come through the village every summer.'

'Not *hundreds*. Maybe one or two. But it wouldn't do any harm to check Dod out though, would it?'

'How do you think you can do that?'

Nora shrugged. 'We could take a walk up by his house when he's out.'

'And break in?'

'He never locks the door, you know that.' Most people in the village didn't, not in the daytime at least.

The bell rang to mark the end of break.

'What do you say?' asked Nora.

'I dunno,' said Lecky.

At lunchtime, Mrs Fraser took the children into the wood to look at the ospreys' nest. They stopped on the edge of the clearing.

'We must keep our distance,' said Mrs Fraser. 'We don't want to upset the birds even more.'

The two parent birds were still there, circling their empty nest. Round and round they went, aimlessly. They looked as if they didn't know what to do with themselves. The sight of them quietened the children.

'They must be hoping somebody will bring their eggs back,' said Nora.

'But they won't,' said Lecky gloomily.

'Poor birds,' said Mrs Fraser.

'They look awfully sad,' said Jessie, her daughter.

'You'd be sad if your babies got stolen,' said Nora.

'Won't they have any more?' asked Claire.

'Not this year,' said Lecky. 'And Dad says they might not even come back to nest here next year.'

'I wish those thieves would come back here right now!' said Nora.

'We could trip them up,' said Rod Smith, sticking out his foot to show how he would do it.

'And tie them up!' said Tommy Rankin, lassooing them with an imaginary rope.

'And drag them along to the police station!' said Nora.

'That'd be right!' said Lecky. 'I could just see you!'

'We've got to do something about these egg thieves,' said Nora.

'There's not much we can do this year. It's too late.'

'We could start a protection society of our own.'

'Hey, that's a good idea!' said Tommy.

'Yes, I think it would be a good idea,' said Mrs Fraser.

They turned as they heard heavy feet crackling on fallen branches. Two men were coming their way. But it wasn't the egg thieves returning to the scene of their crime. It was a reporter from the local paper and a photographer with a heavy camera hanging round his neck.

The photographer had come to photograph the tree and the nest and the two unhappy parent birds. He took quite a while doing it, taking them from this angle and that. He even lay on his back on the ground.

The reporter interviewed Lecky. It must have been the tenth time he'd told his story!

'So how do you kids feel about this?' asked the reporter, his pen poised above his pad. 'Can you give me a quote?'

'We're furious!' said Nora.

The reporter wrote that down.

'It's like getting your house burgled,' said Claire. Her auntie's house in Glasgow had been burgled a week or two back. Her auntie hadn't had a wink of sleep since.

'We're planning to set up our own osprey protection society,' said Nora.

The reporter was scribbling away.

'We're going to stop them doing this again!' vowed Lecky.

'They'll not get away with it another time!' cried Nora.

On the way back to school, she said to Lecky, 'What about Dod Smith?'

'What about him? You've only got old Mr Taylor's gossip to go on.'

'I suppose you're right,' sighed Nora.

They forgot all about Dod Smith, in the meantime.

Chapter Three

ANGRY CHILDREN SET UP
OSPREY WATCH!

So ran the headline in the paper when it came out the following Thursday. The paper was published only once a week.

Mrs Fraser read the article aloud to them: 'Local children are so angry that the ospreys' eggs have been stolen that they have vowed to set up a protection society. They said they were determined to stop the egg thieves from stealing the eggs next year.'

She pinned the cutting on the noticeboard and the children wrote stories and poems about the ospreys. The first and second year infants drew pictures of men pulling eggs from the nest. The men in their drawings had enormous heads, bulging eyes and long, snaky fingers. All the work was put up on the wall.

After a while the pictures and stories came down to make way for new ones, but the newspaper cutting stayed on the board throughout the summer and the following winter. It was looking a bit yellow and frayed at the edges by the time March blew in wild and windy. Snow fell on the hills, but melted quickly down in the village. The ospreys usually came back at the beginning of April.

The children began to talk again about their protection society.

'We ought to build a hide,' said Lecky.

The older children went into the wood after school. When they arrived at the clearing they saw that the ospreys' nest had been damaged by the winter storms. Part of one side was hanging out.

'They won't want to come back to that, will they?' said Nora.

'If they do come back they'll mend it,' said Lecky.

Mr Grant helped them choose a spot for the hide, well back from the nest. He picked a slightly raised mound some thirty metres away. When he stood on top of it he could see the nest through his binoculars.

'Yes, this would be a good spot.'

The wood here was ramshackle.

Several old trees had had their trunks split in the high winds. Others had been completely blown down. Branches lay higgledy-piggledy over the ground, making it difficult to pick a way through.

They set to work. They cleared a space, then using fallen branches and some strong sacking material they made a tent-like structure in the shelter of two or three young, low trees.

'It looks a bit like one of those Indian teepees,' said Tommy.

The hide would hold two comfortably, three at a pinch.

'We'll take it in turns to watch,' said Lecky.

'We could draw up a rota,' suggested Tommy.

'A good idea,' said Nora.

'We can't be here *all* the time though, can we?' said Claire. 'My mum wouldn't let me come in the morning while it's still dark.'

'My dad will be keeping a look-out as well,' said Lecky.

'So will mine,' said Calum Murray, whose father was the police constable.

'That didn't stop them before, did it?' said Nora.

'But this year *everybody* will be watching for thieves!' said Lecky.

April came in, still windy and wet, but the daffodils were out and a few purple and yellow crocuses peeked through the hard ground. The first lambs were born and starting to stagger about on wobbly legs in the field at the back of the school wall.

The children waited anxiously for any sign of the ospreys. The first day of the first week passed. And the second day. And the third.

'They may not come back,' Mr Grant reminded them. 'You have to be prepared for that.'

Lecky rose early every morning and sat at his window with his binoculars. He kept them trained on the wood.

On the fifth day he made a sighting.

'Dad,' he yelled, running into his parents' room, 'the ospreys are back!'

He knew it would be the male bird.

He always came back first to check on the nest or to begin building a new one.

Lecky didn't say anything in class that day as he didn't want everyone to go barging into the wood to disturb the osprey.

'What are you up to today?' asked Nora.

'Nothing.' He tried to look innocent.

'You keep smiling to yourself,' she said suspiciously.

'What's wrong with smiling?' he asked.

He hurried home after school, giving Nora the slip. His father was waiting for him. They took their binoculars and went cautiously into the wood, taking care to make as little noise as possible. They slipped into the hide.

The osprey was flying in wide circles high above his old nest, clearly visible against the blue and white of the sky. He was displaying the full span of his wings. He looked magnificent, flying away up there above the treetops.

'He's showing off,' said Mr Grant softly. 'He must be nearly three hundred metres up! He's telling the world — stay away from my space!'

Someone was coming. Someone with coppery red hair. It was Nora! Who else? Lecky groaned. She was trying to walk on tiptoe, but her feet were making the fallen branches crackle and snap.

'Be quiet!' he whispered.

'No need to shout!'

He glared at her, but he moved over to make room. His dad let her look through his binoculars. She'd just got them between her hands when the osprey flew off.

'He's gone!' she cried. And Lecky would probably blame her for chasing him away!

'He'll be back, I expect,' said Mr Grant. 'He may have gone for nesting material.'

'That would mean he intends to stay!' said Lecky excitedly.

They waited patiently and ten minutes later the osprey returned with a long stick clenched firmly in his talons. It looked like a piece of dead branch.

He began to fly in wide circles again, as he had done before, high above his eyrie. Then, suddenly, he climbed even higher, making fast wing beats. He gave a high-pitched call. He hovered. Now he was diving rapidly down. He landed on the nest.

The three watchers sighed with relief. The bird's head twitched. He was listening and watching. The stick he was holding must

have been nearly a metre long. After a few minutes he seemed to decide it was safe to start work. He began by pitching out the old lining. Mr Grant raised his thumb in triumph and Lecky and Nora grinned at each other. They stayed for an hour in the hide and then went back to the village to spread the good news.

The following day, the female osprey returned. She was even bigger than the male. Both birds would have spent the winter in West Africa.

'But not together,' said Mr Grant.

'Gosh!' Nora found that amazing. 'Do you mean they haven't seen one another since the end of last summer?'

'That's right.'

And yet they had found each other, just like that.

'And their nest,' said Mr Grant.

'They're so clever,' said Nora. Imagine

finding the way back from Africa to this particular wood, to this particular tree! She and Lecky had almost got lost in the wood once and they'd known it ever since they could walk.

The birds were busy, intent on the task in hand. They were rebuilding their home. They flew to and fro, to and fro, carrying bits of bark, moss and turf for the lining of the nest. From time to time the male bird went off to fish. Lecky's dad told them that ospreys would travel to lochs and rivers up to ten miles away. When the bird brought a fish back, his mate joined him in a nearby tree for the feast. They never ate in the nest.

'I'm going to call them Oona and Ollie,' said Nora. The names caught on.

At school that week, all the drawings on the wall were of ospreys: ospreys in full flight with wings expanded; ospreys repairing their nest; ospreys diving for fish in the river.

'I think you should stay away from the wood until the nest is built and the female has laid her eggs,' said Mrs Fraser.

At the end of the month Lecky and his dad saw the female osprey sitting on the nest.

'It seems Oona's laid an egg!' said Lecky, when he came into school that morning. 'She'll not budge much now. And when she does Ollie will keep guard.'

The children were excited. They drew nests with one large egg sitting in the centre. Osprey eggs were white with chocolate-coloured splotches and, surprisingly, no larger than hens' eggs.

In the next few days Mr Grant

thought the female might have laid two more eggs. He decided to go up the tree to look. He took the long pole again, with the mirror on the end of it. While he was up the tree Oona flew off and squawked and flapped around but she settled down quickly again afterwards.

'There are three eggs there,' Mr Grant confirmed.

Lecky brought the news to school again and recorded it in the diary. 'It'll take thirty-five to forty days for them to hatch.'

'That's an awful lot of days to wait,' groaned Claire. 'More than a month.'

'And it's an awful lot of days for the egg thieves to strike!' said Nora.

'Yes,' agreed Lecky, 'now is the dangerous time. We must start our watch.'

Chapter Four

'Dod Smith seems to be in the money these days,' commented Mrs McPhee.

'What did you say?' demanded Nora, pricking up her ears.

It was Saturday morning and she was in the shop giving her mother a hand. She liked being in the shop and having the chance to chat to people as they came in and out. There was usually a bit of bustle on Saturdays.

'Usually he hasn't two pennies to rub

together.' Mrs McPhee then broke off to say, 'Don't just sit there reading those comics, Nora! Get them out on the shelf. And I'm not wanting them all creased before you do.'

'So usually Dod doesn't have two pennies to rub together,' she reminded her mother.

'It's just that he seems to be spending a lot these days,' said Mrs McPhee, with an eye on her husband who was at the back of the post office counter. 'He bought a new TV last week. The delivery man called here to ask the way to his house.'

At that point the door opened and in came Dod himself.

'Dod!' exclaimed Nora in surprise.

Her mother gave her a look which said, *Don't be saying anything about his TV!*

'How are you doing, Nora?' asked Dod.

'Fine,' she replied, eyeing his sweater, which she could see beneath his open anorak. It was bright scarlet, which matched his woollen hat, and it looked brand new. The hat wasn't new. It had seen many a winter. Dod and new clothes didn't seem to go together. Nora had only ever seen him in a shabby old khaki-coloured jersey, scruffy trousers and tackity boots.

'I like your sweater,' she said.

'Do you?' He was pleased. 'I got it in the town last Saturday.'

'Are you going to town today?'

'I am indeed. I'm getting the eleven bus.'

It was ten-to now.

'I've come in for some mints. I like a sweetie to suck on the bus.'

Nora served him.

'Have you any shopping to get in the town today?' she asked casually. At least she was *trying* to sound casual.

'I might get myself a pair of trousers. You know those kind with all the pockets down the legs?'

'They'd be handy right enough,' put in Mrs McPhee.

'That's what I think. I could keep all my bits and pieces in them.'

Dod took his mints and went out to wait for the bus.

'He does seem to be in the money, doesn't he?' said Nora.

The bus came along in the next few minutes. She watched through the window as Dod clambered aboard, the pom-pom on top of his hat bobbing busily.

'Do you need me now?' she asked, sliding out from behind the counter.

'I suppose you're wanting away,' said her mother.

Nora pulled on her anorak. 'Won't be long.'

The street was empty, now that the bus had gone. She walked quickly, passing old Mr Taylor's long, low cottage without a sideways glance, then the pub, then Claire's house, which was set back a bit from the road, and then the church and the manse. The minister was standing at his door. She gave him a wave but didn't stop. She didn't want to waste any time. When she reached the end of the street she broke into a run.

Lecky lived half a mile down the road. He was at home.

'He's upstairs working on his aeroplane model,' said his mother, who was baking scones. The smell made Nora's mouth water. Lecky's mother was the best baker in the village. She always took first prize at the cake baking competitions at the fête. Nora's own mum didn't have time to bake, with being in the shop all day.

Lecky was absorbed in his aeroplane kit. 'Hang on a minute,' he cried. 'I'm at a tricky part.'

Nora moved from one foot to the other as he glued the part into place.

'OK,' he said finally.

'You remember I told you Mr Taylor thought Dod Smith might be the one who leaked the ospreys' nest to the egg thieves?'

'Not that again!'

'No, wait, Lecky!' Nora told him about Dod coming in to money. 'So don't you think we should go and check him out?'

'And what do you think we would find?'

'I dunno. But maybe something.'

'You're off the wall, Nora McPhee.'

'I am not, Lecky Grant! Well, I'm going up to his house.' Nora tossed her head. 'You needn't come if you don't want to.'

'I guess I'd better. To see you don't do anything stupid!'

She knew he'd come. He'd be too curious not to.

Mrs Grant gave them a hot scone dripping with butter and they left, saying they were going for a walk. They took the road that went up behind the village.

On the way they met PC Murray in his car. He stopped and put his head out of the window.

'What are you two up to this morning?' he asked.

'Nothing,' said Nora.

'Bird watching, I'll bet, if I know Lecky!'

He didn't wait for an answer, but went rolling on down the hill. There was no one else about and no noise but for the sound of the wind and the calling of the sheep. Dod's cottage stood alone, well away from any other.

They slid over the dyke and crossed the stretch of moorland that led to it, dodging the sheep. Dod kept only a few, as well as a couple of goats and some chickens, which were pecking at the ground close to the house.

'It's against the law, you know,' said Lecky, 'breaking into someone's house.'

'We won't have to break in,' said Nora. 'Not if the door's open.'

It wasn't.

'That's funny.' Nora frowned. 'He doesn't usually lock the door, I know he doesn't. My dad brings shopping up for him and he just opens the door and puts it in.'

'Maybe he felt like locking it today.'

'Maybe he had something to hide! I wonder where he's left the key.'

Nora looked under a boulder lying close by. It wasn't there. Lecky kicked aside a few other stones.

'Probably took it with him,' he said.

'It must be a big key. To fit that lock . . .'

Nora went round the side. She bent down. 'Got it!' she cried. The key was tucked behind the pipe where it came down to the drain.

'We're still not having to break in,' she said, fitting the key in the lock.

'But it's trespassing.'

'You chicken?'

'You joking?' Lecky went in ahead of her.

It was dark inside the house. Something leapt out of a doorway and Nora jumped and screamed.

'It's only a cat, stupid!' said Lecky.

They went into the living room-cum-kitchen. The place was in a terrible mess. Dirty dishes and pots littered the draining board and table. The floor was covered with old newspapers, socks, boots and cat dishes. The furniture was ancient and tatty.

'What a pong!' Nora wrinkled her nose.

'He never opens the windows,' said Lecky.

Nora began to hunt vaguely around.

'What is it that you think you're looking for?' asked Lecky.

'Evidence.'

'Evidence!' He snorted. 'All this tells us is that Dod's no good at housework.' He kept watch at the window in case someone might be coming. At the moment all he could see were sheep grazing on the bits of grass in between the heather.

Suddenly he straightened up. 'Hey, Nora, it's the postie!'

They hadn't reckoned on Dod getting mail. The red post van was coming bumping up the rough track towards the house.

'We'll have to hide,' said Nora.

Lecky opened a door. It led into the coal cellar, though there were only a few bits of coal in it. Dod would mostly burn logs that he stored outside. The cupboard smelt strongly of coal. They had no choice. The postie was slamming the door of his van. They crammed themselves into the cupboard and pulled the door shut. It was pitch black inside and there was no air.

'Can't breathe,' said Nora.

'Too bad,' said Lecky.

The front door was opening.

'Dod?' called the postie. 'Are you there, Doddie? I've got a parcel for you.'

They heard the postie's feet coming along the passage and into the room. He must be standing only a metre or two from them!

Nora thought she would explode. The smell of the coal dust was making her feel sick and her nose was prickling like mad. She could feel a huge sneeze building up. She pinched her nostrils tightly between her fingers. If she didn't get out of here soon she would throw up, or faint.

Then the footsteps moved away. The front door closed. Lecky opened the cupboard door a crack letting in light and air. They listened. They heard the sound of an engine.

'He's going,' said Lecky.

They emerged from the coal cellar. Nora let out an enormous sneeze. Then she began to laugh.

'Look at you, Lecky Grant, you're all sooty!'

'Look at yourself, Nora McPhee! Talk about the pot calling the kettle black!'

'The postie left Dod's parcel,' said Nora.

It was a bulky package.

'Don't touch it!' warned Lecky as she went to lift it. 'You'll make it dirty.'

'Looks like something ordered out of a catalogue,' said Nora. 'It *is* amazing that Dod can suddenly buy so much stuff.'

'Come on, let's go!' said Lecky. 'Before anyone else comes.'

'But we haven't had a proper look round.'

'There's nothing to see.'

Nora peeked under a cushion on the seat of an armchair.

'What's this?' she cried.

She wiped her hands on her jeans and pulled out an envelope. It crackled. It wasn't sealed. She lifted the flap. They looked inside.

'Money,' said Lecky in a whisper.

'A lot of money.'

They counted it. It came to two hundred pounds. Where *would* Dod get two hundred pounds?

Chapter Five

They puzzled over Dod's two hundred pounds all week, but there was no way that they could find out how he'd got it. Even Nora didn't have enough cheek to ask him. He was going about the village in his new trousers, showing everyone all the different pockets he had. Nora admired them.

'They're great, aren't they?' He grinned. He had a spanner in one pocket and some rusty nails in another.

'Are you going shopping this Saturday?' she asked.

'I'm not sure that I'll be needing anything.'

On Saturday morning, Nora was again in the shop. Dod didn't come in. The eleven o'clock bus came and went.

A little while later, a strange car pulled up in front of the post office. Nora craned her neck to see. A man and a woman were getting out. She'd never seen them before. They glanced around the street for a moment or two then they came into the shop.

'We believe there's an osprey nest in the area?' said the woman in a chatty voice.

'Couldn't tell you,' said Mrs McPhee, who was sorting a box of chocolate bars. She didn't look up.

The man leaned on the counter. 'You

must have some idea where it is?'

'We're very keen bird watchers, you see.' The woman gave a big smile that was wasted on Mrs McPhee.

'Sorry I can't help you,' she said.

Nora kept her eye on them. They often did have people coming in to ask about the ospreys and they never let on to them that they knew where the nest was. But she didn't think they'd be so open about it if they were thieves. You never knew, though, did you?

The couple left. Nora watched them as they got back into their car and drove off. She snaffled a chocolate bar and drifted up the street after them. They'd gone only a little way down the road and parked in a lay-by beside the wood.

They hailed her. 'Hello there, dear!' said the woman.

'We're really keen to find the ospreys,' said the man.

'You wouldn't know where they are, would you?' asked the woman.

'I think it's over that way.' Nora pointed across the road, on the opposite side from the nest.

The man turned to the woman. 'What do you think?'

'Might as well give it a go.'

'Thanks,' said the man to Nora.

They disappeared into the wood, taking the direction she had suggested. She smiled. She heard the couple crashing about between the trees. They certainly weren't true bird watchers, not if they went stumbling about like that. They'd scare anything off for miles.

She called at Lecky's house and his mother said he'd gone into the wood. 'He's been in there most of the day!'

Nora remembered that she was supposed to be in the hide with him that morning! It was on the rota. They'd been keeping watch after school every day, but there'd been nothing out of the way to report. The female was sitting on the nest and the male was bringing back food.

Nora found Lecky in the hide. She got in beside him and told him about the man and woman.

'They're probably just curious,' said Lecky.

Nora nodded. She broke her chocolate bar in two and passed half to him. They munched quietly and took turns to watch through the binoculars. Oona was on the nest. There was no sign of Ollie.

'He's probably gone fishing,' said Lecky.

Oona seemed a bit disturbed.

'What's up with her?' asked Nora.

'Don't know.' Lecky frowned.

Oona was moving around. She appeared to be pecking at something.

'It's an egg!' said Lecky.

'She's not eating it, is she?'

'I think it must be damaged. She's testing it to find out.'

Oona pecked for another minute or two, then she took the egg into her beak and flew to a neighbouring tree.

'What's she going to do?' cried Nora.

Oona looked down at the ground, opened her beak and dropped the egg.

'Oh no!' cried Nora.

'It must have been cracked,' said Lecky sadly.

Oona flew back to the nest and squatted on the remaining eggs.

'Now there are only two,' said Nora.

'Let's hope no more get damaged!' said Lecky.

'Or stolen,' said Nora. 'It's not easy for them, is it? Having babies?'

They were about to go home for lunch when they heard someone coming. It didn't sound like the couple who'd been in the car. This person was treading carefully, trying not to make a noise.

They saw a movement through the branches. They thought it might be a man wearing a dark green jacket. A lot of people wore green jackets, especially in the country. He wasn't close enough for them to make him out properly. He was heading in the direction of the ospreys' nest. Now he was stopping. He was making no noise at all. Lecky and Nora made none either.

They stayed like that for a few minutes, afraid almost to breathe, then they heard him again. He was coming back. This time he passed closer to the hide.

When he came into their sight-line they saw that the man was Dod Smith and that he had a pair of binoculars round his neck.

Lecky and Nora crept out of the hide. They followed him out of the wood and up the road, keeping a good distance between them. Dod stopped in the village and went into the phone box.

'He's phoning someone!' said Nora excitedly.

'Could be anybody,' said Lecky.

'Could be an egg thief!'

They hovered around until he'd finished his call. When he came out of the box Nora called over to him.

'Hi, Dod!'

'Oh, hello, didn't see you there!'

'Are those new binoculars that you've got?' she asked Nora.

'I just got them yesterday. From one of those catalogue things. Through the mail, you know. Want to see?'

He unstrapped the case and took out the glasses. He allowed each of them to look through the lenses in turn.

'They're really good ones!' said Lecky.

'We saw you in the wood, Dod,' said Nora.

'I was just trying the binoculars out. Taking a wee look at the birds.'

'At the ospreys?' said Nora.

'Aye, the ospreys. Great looking birds.'

Dod put the binoculars back in their case and set off up the hill whistling.

'He must have come into a fortune,' said Lecky.

'Or else someone's paying him for information,' said Nora.

Chapter Six

They were all quite jumpy now about
the eggs. There were still a lot of days
to go before they would hatch out. The
nights were moonlit, a good time for
thieves to strike. Lecky found it difficult
to get to sleep at nights. Every time he
heard a noise he jumped up and went
to the window. Every time a strange car
came through the village the children
stared after it as if it might contain the
thieves. If they could, they noted down

the registration number. Nora kept a notebook on the shop counter to record the numbers.

Lecky's dad rose early each morning to go into the wood and check the nest.

'So far, so good,' he'd report at breakfast time.

On Sunday evening, Mr Grant had to go and visit his mother. She'd rung to say she wasn't feeling well and could he come over. She lived thirty miles away.

'Want to come with me, Lecky?' he asked.

'I said I'd play table tennis.'

Mr Grant told his wife that he shouldn't be too late back.

Lecky went along to Nora's house, which was attached to the post office. She had a table tennis table set up in her garage. Her mum and dad kept their car in the street, except in mid-winter when it snowed or the frosts were severe.

Calum and Claire arrived soon after Lecky to make up a foursome. They left the door of the garage open on to the street for air. They played a few games and then took a break.

While they were drinking the Coke that Nora's mother had handed in, they saw a car sweep past. Not many cars came through the village on a Sunday evening.

'Strangers,' said Nora, going out into the street to gaze after it. 'Dark car.'

'Too early in the evening for egg thieves,' said Lecky.

'They might think they'd fool us by coming early,' said Nora. 'I mean, you wouldn't *expect* them at this time, would you?'

'She's right,' said Calum. 'And it *is* just

beginning to get dark.'

'I think we should check them out.' Nora put down her Coke can. 'Make sure they've gone.'

Claire had to go home. Her granny was visiting for the night and would want to see her. The others accompanied Claire as far as her house, then went on through the village. The street was dead. Not even a cat was on the move. Most people would be inside watching television.

They carried on down the road, past the church and the manse. When they turned the first corner they couldn't see any sign of the car.

'They could have parked round the next bend,' said Nora.

'They could have parked ten miles away!' said Lecky.

They walked on, anyway.

Suddenly Lecky shouted, 'Get down!' They flattened themselves on the ground.

Up ahead, two men in dark clothes had rounded the bend and were coming  towards them. They were keeping close to the trees, skirting the edge of the wood.

Lecky raised his head a little to get a better look. 'I don't think they saw us. They're making for the path into the wood!'

'That will take them straight to the nest!' said Nora.

'They're going into the wood now!' Lecky jumped up.

'Looks like they could be our egg thieves!' cried Nora.

'We've got to stop them before they get to the eggs!' said Lecky. 'You'd better go for your dad, Calum. Pity mine's away!' The Grants' house was closer than the police officer's.

'Tell your dad two men are acting suspiciously in the wood, Calum,' urged Nora.

'Tell him to come quickly,' added Lecky. 'And to bring someone else with him if he can!' There were *two* men, after all.

Calum sprinted off.

'We'll cut into the wood from here,' said Lecky. 'They might have a look-out on the track.' He led the way in through the trees, pushing aside overhanging branches. Nora followed.

'No talking, now!' he warned.

'You don't have to tell me, Lecky Grant!'

The route they were taking was more difficult than their usual one. There was no definite path to follow. They had to climb over felled trees and scramble under fallen branches. But Lecky knew the wood well. He could have found his way blindfold.

They stopped for a moment to listen. The faint rustling noises they could hear might be made by men or animals. Deer roamed freely in the wood.

Lecky nodded to Nora and they moved on. He was aiming to come into the right of the ospreys' tree. Every few steps he paused to glance up, to check whether the nest was in sight. The moon was out now, lighting up the treetops.

He drew in a sharp breath and stopped so abruptly that Nora almost tripped on his heels. He grabbed her arm to quieten her and pointed at the sky. Looking up, she saw what he had seen. Ollie was in flight, high overhead, veering in wide circles, flapping his wings and giving forth frantic cries.

'Maybe we're too late!' cried Nora.

'Come on!' yelled Lecky and he went crashing off through the undergrowth. Nora dashed after him.

They reached the clearing in time to see a man in the process of climbing the osprey tree. They saw him clearly in the white moonlight. He was dressed in black from head to foot. A balaclava covered his head. He was about ten feet from the ground, just above the barbed wire.

Chapter Seven

'Get off!' screamed Lecky. 'Leave that nest alone!'

The man looked down, startled. They'd taken him by surprise. He stayed motionless for a few seconds leaning his body in against the trunk of the tree, as if he were uncertain as to what to do next. Ollie was continuing to squawk loudly overhead, with Oona joining in from the nest. She hadn't yet abandoned it.

'Get down!' cried Lecky again.

The noise had alerted the other man, who must have been on the look-out further down the path. He came running. The one on the tree began to climb again.

'Oh, no!' groaned Nora. 'Hang in there, Oona!'

The look-out was also dressed in black and wearing a balaclava. They couldn't see his face, only his eyes glittering in the slit. That was the most terrifying part of him. They were so frightened that they felt stuck to the ground. He stood in front of them, towering above them.

'Get out of here, you kids!' he commanded. 'Fast! If you know what's good for you!'

'The police are coming,' said Lecky.

'Don't give me that!'

At that moment they heard shouts and the sound of feet drumming on the path.

'They're coming!' cried Nora. 'They are!'

The man on the ground spun round. He hesitated, but only for a second before deciding to make a run for it. He went headlong into the trees.

They turned to see what the man up the tree would do. He was holding on to the trunk still but leaning out from it. Now he jumped! He came flying down through the air like a great heavy black bird. The children stood back.

As he was picking himself up, Nora put out her foot and tripped him. He went sprawling face down on the ground. She raised her arms above her head and cheered.

By now PC Murray had arrived, panting, in the clearing, followed by

Calum and four other men from the village whom he'd collected on the way. Both Nora's and Lecky's fathers were amongst them. Mr Grant had just returned from visiting his mother.

'So this is one of them, I presume,' said PC Murray, hauling the man to his feet and clipping on handcuffs.

'It is,' said Lecky.

'He was up the tree,' said Nora.

PC Murray pulled the balaclava down off the man's face. No one there had ever seen him before.

'The other man ran off,' said Nora. 'He went that way. Into the wood.'

'He'll not find his way out of there very easily,' said Mr Grant. 'That part's a bit of a jungle.'

'We think they might have parked their car further on down the road,' said Lecky. 'Round the bend. He might try to make for that.'

'Right, lads!' said PC Murray. 'Let's go and find it!'

They found the car before the runaway did. It was the car the children had seen earlier. The thieves had left it on the edge of the wood, just off the road.

'He must still be wandering about in the wood,' said Lecky.

'Serve him right!' said Nora. 'Horrible man!'

The handcuffed man was saying nothing. He was keeping his head down and his eyes on the ground.

'You should be away home to your bed, Nora,' said her father.

But she didn't go and he didn't make her. Other people from the village had come out now and were gathered in the road. News always travelled fast.

It was almost an hour later before the

second thief emerged from the wood. He looked bedraggled. Bits of branch and bark clung to his balaclava. He seemed astounded to see such a crowd awaiting him. He was about to turn and run again when he thought better of it. After all, where could he go?

'Come quietly, sir,' said PC Murray. 'I'm arresting you both for attempting to steal eggs from the osprey nest in this wood.'

The man came quietly and took off his balaclava when instructed. He, too, stared at the ground.

Mr Grant was eyeing him and frowning. 'Hey, I know you, don't I?'

The man looked up.

'You drive a truck for one of the forestry's timber contractors! So that's how you know about our nest!'

Nora and Lecky looked at each other. They were both thinking the same thing. They'd been wrong about Dod!

PC Murray was radioing for help to the police station in the town. He couldn't cope on his own with two arrests. A couple of constables came in a squad car and took the men away. The villagers made their way home. PC Murray said the men would get probably get very heavy fines. 'The last ones to be caught were fined a few thousand.'

In the morning, at first light, Lecky and his father went back into the woods to see how the ospreys were faring after their adventure. Oona was sitting on the nest and Ollie was keeping close watch.

'They should be all right now,' said Mr Grant. 'Though we'll still need to keep an eye open in case there are any other thieves about.'

In school they wrote stories and drew pictures of PC Murray arresting the egg thieves. The little children drew enormous pairs of handcuffs.

At lunchtime, Nora went home and returned with a round tin.

'What's in there?' asked Lecky.

'A chocolate cake. I made it yesterday. It's got hundreds and thousands and chocolate buttons on top. I'm going to give it to Dod. I feel awful about suspecting him. And he was innocent all the time!'

'I suspected him too, didn't I?'

'But it was me that started it,' she said miserably.

Lecky went with her after school. Dod was pottering about outside his door.

'Dod,' said Nora, presenting him with the tin, 'this is for you.'

'For me?' He lifted the lid and looked inside. 'A *cake*? You're giving it to *me*?'

Nora nodded.

'Nobody's ever given me a cake before. How did you know it was my birthday? You must have second sight!'

Nora did not deny it. She avoided Lecky's eye. For of course she hadn't known it was Dod's birthday.

'Come on in,' he said. 'And I'll make you a wee cup of tea.'

They had seen the state of his kitchen so they weren't too keen on the idea of a cup of tea. But they went in anyway.

Dod's tea tasted like tar. They sipped it slowly from thick, cracked mugs. He put the cake on a plate and cut it with a knife that he kept for gutting fish. They each had a slice.

'That's fantastic cake, Nora!' said Dod. 'The best I've ever eaten. How do you like my new teapot?' He held it up for them to admire. It was blue, and decorated with red roses. 'Pretty, eh?'

Lecky nodded. His mouth was too full of sticky chocolate sponge to speak. The cake wasn't bad though, considering Nora had made it.

'You've been treating yourself quite a bit lately, Dod,' said Nora.

He chuckled. 'I have that. Will I let you into a secret?'

'Please!'

'I had a win on the lottery last year! Not a big win, you understand, but big enough for me. A few thousand.'

'A few thousand!' echoed Nora. She would call that big.

'Wow!' said Lecky.

'You did manage to keep it secret, didn't you?' said Nora.

'You'll not be telling, will you? I'm not wanting the whole village to know. They'd be up here trying to borrow money from me.'

'Don't worry, Dod,' said Nora, 'I promise you I'll never ever tell! Cross my heart!'

'And you'd better not tell anyone!' said Lecky when they were going back down the hill afterwards.

'I won't!' said Nora indignantly. 'Of course I won't! Dod's our friend now, isn't he?'

Two weeks later, two osprey chicks were safely hatched. Their birth was recorded in the school diary. Everyone in the village was delighted. The talk in the shop was of nothing else.

Lecky and Nora went up to Dod's house after school and asked him if he'd like to come down to their hide to look at the ospreys.

'Thanks very much,' he said. 'I'd like that fine.'

He fetched his new binoculars. Lecky had brought his with him and Nora had borrowed her father's.

They crept quietly into the hide. There was just room for the three of them, with a bit of a squash. They trained their binoculars on the hide.

Oona was on the nest.

'Do you see the babies' beaks sticking up?' asked Lecky.

'Aye,' nodded Dod, 'I do.'

'Oh, look!' whispered Nora excitedly. 'Oona's just popped a bit of fish into one of the beaks! Gobble, gobble, it's gone!'

'That's a great sight!' said Dod.

'It is, isn't it?' said Lecky happily.

'They're safe from those horrible men now,' said Nora with a sigh.

'You should get a medal,' declared Dod. 'You should! The two of you. For catching the egg thieves.'

Coaching Youth Soccer

FIFTH EDITION

American Sport Education Program with Sam Snow

Human Kinetics

Library of Congress Cataloging-in-Publication Data

Coaching youth soccer / American Sport Education Program ; with Sam Snow. -- 5th ed.
   p. cm.
 ISBN-13: 978-0-7360-9217-3 (soft cover)
 ISBN-10: 0-7360-9217-X (soft cover)
 1. Soccer for children--Coaching. 2. Soccer--Coaching. I. Snow, Sam. II. American Sport Education Program.
 GV943.8.C63 2011
 796.33407'7--dc22

                              2011002858

ISBN-10: 0-7360-9217-X (print)
ISBN-13: 978-0-7360-9217-3 (print)

The Web addresses cited in this text were current as of April 2011 unless otherwise noted.

Content Provider: Sam Snow, US Youth Soccer Coaching Director; **Acquisitions Editors:** Annie Parrett and Aaron Thais; **Managing Editor:** Laura E. Podeschi; **Assistant Editor:** Tyler Wolpert; **Copyeditor:** Patricia MacDonald; **Permission Manager:** Martha Gullo; **Graphic Designer:** Nancy Rasmus; **Graphic Artist:** Tara Welsch; **Cover Designer:** Keith Blomberg; **Photographer (cover):** © Human Kinetics; **Photographer (interior):** Neil Bernstein, unless otherwise noted; photos on pp. 1, 9, 19, 31, 49, 87, 121, 139, 161, and 173 © Human Kinetics; **Photo Asset Manager:** Laura Fitch; **Visual Production Assistant:** Joyce Brumfield; **Photo Production Manager:** Jason Allen; **Art Manager:** Kelly Hendren; **Associate Art Manager:** Alan L. Wilborn; **Illustrations:** © Human Kinetics; **Printer:** Edwards Brothers

We thank Pizza Hut Park in Frisco, Texas, for assistance in providing the location for the photo shoot for this book.

Copies of this book are available at special discounts for bulk purchase for sales promotions, premiums, fund-raising, or educational use. Special editions or book excerpts can also be created to specifications. For details, contact the Special Sales Manager at Human Kinetics.

Printed in the United States of America   10 9 8 7 6 5 4 3 2 1

The paper in this book is certified under a sustainable forestry program.

Human Kinetics
Web site: www.HumanKinetics.com

United States: Human Kinetics
P.O. Box 5076
Champaign, IL 61825-5076
800-747-4457
e-mail: humank@hkusa.com

Canada: Human Kinetics
475 Devonshire Road Unit 100
Windsor, ON N8Y 2L5
800-465-7301 (in Canada only)
e-mail: info@hkcanada.com

Europe: Human Kinetics
107 Bradford Road
Stanningley
Leeds LS28 6AT, United Kingdom
+44 (0) 113 255 5665
e-mail: hk@hkeurope.com

Australia: Human Kinetics
57A Price Avenue
Lower Mitcham, South Australia 5062
08 8372 0999
e-mail: info@hkaustralia.com

New Zealand: Human Kinetics
P.O. Box 80
Torrens Park, South Australia 5062
0800 222 062
e-mail: info@hknewzealand.com

E5120

To my parents, who as managers, teachers, and coaches themselves gave me the education, experiences, and patient support that allowed me to become a professional coach.

Contents

Foreword   vi
Welcome to Coaching   viii
Welcome From US Youth Soccer   ix
Activity Finder   x
Key to Diagrams   xii

1 Stepping Into Coaching   1

2 Communicating as a Coach   9

3 Understanding Rules and Equipment   19

4 Providing for Players' Safety   31

5 Making Training Sessions
  Fun and Practical   49

6 Teaching and Shaping Skills   75

7 Attacking   87

8 Defending   121

9 Goalkeeping   139

10 Coaching on Match Day   161

11 Developing Season
and Training Plans   173

Appendix   189
Glossary   195
About the Authors   201

Foreword

The status of the US national soccer teams suggests that we still have improvements to make in our approach to developing players. The fundamental problems begin at the youth level, where our time with ball is so limited and our ideas on what to do in training are so ordinary. The rest of the world escapes us because what is apparent once we get to a senior level is our lack of comfort with the ball at our feet. Some of the solutions to the challenges that players of both sexes face are provided in this excellent book by Sam Snow.

I've had the extraordinary privilege of spending a week observing Barcelona close up, watching them compete against Arsenal, then seeing the first team train, and then spending the rest of the time studying their academy program. Every player in the academy, at every age and skill level, demonstrated a tremendous commitment to his or her own development. Equally impressive and telling was what Barca coaches designated their groups to do that day to get better. They emphasized individual skill work and small-sided games, and they encouraged players' love of the ball and the game. Barca coaches also promoted a positive culture of character building, so the conduct of coaches and players and the collective attitudes of everyone were superb. The display of ball mastery and passion for the game were evident, making the entire setting for learning soccer impressive.

So it's no mystery why Spain, with the core of their national team right out of the Barca lineup, is the reigning world champion. This extraordinary game that they play was not built in a day; it was not built with an 11v11 tournament culture like we have here in the United States. And we would do well to learn from that.

Coaching Youth Soccer reflects an understanding of what soccer development in this country should be. It presents advice to help you keep the training fun yet also properly challenging and balanced to help players become comfortable with the ball and make decisions on their own in a climate of player development and mutual respect, like what I observed at Barca. I like Coach Snow's guided discovery approach and small-sided games approach to player improvement. He teaches all the correct principles and presents excellent training games, and his thoughts about the game are up to date.

I have a great fear that the US women are losing ground to Japan, the Koreas (North and South), Brazil, and Germany, countries that have embraced skill development as the foundation for their youth and emphasized a passion for the ball. We need to change our approach to youth soccer development now to catch up and raise our soccer-playing performance to its potential. That effort entails many things on both sides of the gender divide. *Coaching Youth Soccer*, if applied correctly, can play a wonderful part in helping us get there.

Anson Dorrance

Head coach, University of North Carolina women's soccer

21-time national collegiate champion

US women's national coach 1986-1994

1991 FIFA world champion

Welcome to Coaching

Coaching young people is an exciting way to be involved in sport. But it isn't easy. Some coaches are overwhelmed by the responsibilities involved in helping athletes through their early sport experiences. And that's not surprising because coaching youngsters requires more than just showing up. It also involves preparing them physically and mentally to compete effectively, fairly, and safely in their sport and providing them with a positive role model.

This book will help you meet the challenges so you can experience the many rewards of coaching young players. You'll learn how to meet your responsibilities as a coach, communicate well and provide for safety, and teach soccer skills while keeping them fun. More than 40 activities are included throughout the text to help you with your training sessions. We also provide sample practice plans and season plans to guide you throughout your season.

If you would like more information about this or other ASEP resources, please contact us at the following address:

ASEP
P.O. Box 5076
Champaign, IL 61825-5076
800-747-5698
www.ASEP.com

Welcome From US Youth Soccer

Dear Coach,

Welcome to the world of youth soccer. This is your opportunity to have a deep and meaningful impact on young lives. The position of coach is one of influence and prestige in America. You can have a positive influence on your players, both as athletes and as good citizens.

US Youth Soccer and the American Sport Education Program (ASEP) have many resources to assist you in your coaching endeavors. From this book to coaching courses, videos, events, conventions, and online materials, we are here to support your work to create a rich and healthy youth soccer experience.

You hold in your hands a resource you can come back to time and again: *Coaching Youth Soccer*. Whether it's learning how to teach proper fundamental skills or how to communicate better, this book can guide you through your experience of coaching youth soccer.

Here you will find fresh ideas on how to coach children. They may be different from the way you were coached, but these methods are best for grooming passionate players. You will find activities and plenty of resources to aid you in your coaching journey. These coaching methods are based on our experiences in teaching the 300,000 coaches of US Youth Soccer across the USA.

You have at your fingertips a book full of ideas to get you through your first season and many more to come. You will find it easy to follow, an excellent introduction to coaching youth. Between ASEP and US Youth Soccer, you will have access to a wealth of practical information on coaching.

Your coaching will have a profound impression on the players you guide, for today and many years to come. On behalf of the players, thank you for coaching youth soccer!

Keep kicking,

Sam Snow
Technical Director

Activity Finder

	Gamelike activities	
Attacking	Team Tag	Page 56
	Slalom Relay	Page 57
	Single Circular Target	Page 58
	Soccer Marbles	Page 59
	Dribble Attack	Page 60
	Soccer Skittles	Page 61
	The Long Bomb	Page 62
	Heads Up	Page 63
	Hot Potato	Page 64
	Corner Kicking	Page 65
	Throw-In	Page 66
	Obligatory Shooting	Page 67
	Captains	Page 68
Defending	Monkey on Their Backs	Page 69
	The Duel	Page 70
	Crunch Time	Page 71
	Triangular Goal Game	Page 72
Goalkeeping	Narrow Enough	Page 73
	Over the Top	Page 74
	Attacking activities	
Dribbling	Crossing on the Dribble	Page 106
Shooting	Hot Shots	Page 107
	Shooting By Numbers	Page 108
	Mobile Goal Game	Page 109
Receiving	Soccer Tennis	Page 110
	Thighs	Page 111
	Windows	Page 111

Attacking activities		
Passing	Passing Among Teams	Page 112
	Midfield Buildup	Page 113
	Midfield Penetration	Page 114
Tactics	Throw-In at Opposition	Page 115
	Parallel Four-Goal Game	Page 116
	Wingers	Page 117
	Corner Goals Game	Page 118
	All Up in Attack	Page 119
	Two-Ball Game	Page 120
Defending activities		
Marking	Marking Man	Page 130
Tackling	Two Against Two in the Corner	Page 131
	Double Zone	Page 132
Heading	Heading Up	Page 133
Intercepting passes	Interception	Page 134
Making clearances	Neutral Zone	Page 135
Tactics	Handicap Football	Page 136
	Two Open Goals	Page 137
Goalkeeping activities		
Saving shots	What's the Scoop?	Page 156
	Keeper Wars	Page 157
Distributing the ball	Bowling Balls	Page 158
	On the Money	Page 159
	Punting Contest	Page 160

Key to Diagrams

Offensive player

Defensive player

Neutral player

CAP   Captain

CO   Coach

⟶   Player movement

- - - ►   Ball movement

∿∿∿►   Dribble

If you are like most youth soccer coaches, you have probably been recruited from the ranks of concerned parents, soccer enthusiasts, or community volunteers. Like many novice and some veteran coaches, you probably have had little formal instruction on how to coach. But when the call went out for coaches to assist with the local youth soccer club, you answered because you like children and enjoy soccer and perhaps because you want to be involved in a worthwhile community activity.

Your initial coaching assignment may be difficult. Like many volunteers, you may not know everything there is to know about soccer or about how to work with children, especially of varying ages. *Coaching Youth Soccer* will help you learn the basics of coaching soccer effectively. To begin with, we look at the responsibilities you have as a coach. We also talk about what to do when your child is on the team you coach. Finally, we examine five tools for being an effective coach.

> **COACHING TIP**   The development of a soccer player is a long process in which the players progress from a simple to a more complex involvement in the game. This progression requires proper guidance and direction from coaches who are ethical, knowledgeable, and licensed. This process cannot be rushed, but players should participate at a level that is both challenging and demanding. There is no guarantee that players will reach their potential, but you must provide that opportunity!

Your Responsibilities as a Coach

Coaching at any level involves much more than designing set plays for free kicks or drawing up team formations. Coaching involves accepting the tremendous responsibility you face when parents put their children into your care. As a soccer coach, you'll be called on to do the following:

1. Provide a safe physical environment.

Playing soccer holds inherent risks, but as a coach you're responsible for regularly inspecting the practice and game fields and the equipment (see Facilities and Equipment Checklist in the appendix on page 190). Reassure players and parents that, to reduce the chance of injury, you will be teaching the safest techniques and that you have an emergency action plan you will be following (see chapter 4 for more information).

2. Communicate in a positive way.

As you can already see, you have a lot to communicate. You'll communicate not only with your players and parents but also with coaching staff, referees, administrators, and others. Communicate in a positive way that demonstrates you have the best interests of the players at heart (see chapter 2 for more information).

3. Teach the fundamental skills of soccer.

When teaching fundamental skills, keep in mind that soccer is a game; you want to be sure that your players have fun. Therefore, we ask that you help all players be the best they can be by creating a fun, yet productive, training environment. To help you do so, we'll show you an innovative, games-based approach to teaching and practicing the tactics and skills young players need to know—an approach that kids thoroughly enjoy (see chapter 5 for more information). Additionally, to help your players improve their skills, you need to have a sound understanding of attacking, defending, and goalkeeping skills (see chapters 7, 8, and 9).

4. Teach the rules of soccer.

Introduce the rules of soccer, and incorporate them into individual instruction (see chapter 3). You can teach many rules in the first practice, during the course of gamelike activities and small-sided games. Plan to review the rules, however, any time an opportunity naturally arises in training.

5. Direct players in competition.

Match direction includes determining starting lineups and a substitution plan, relating appropriately to referees and to opposing coaches and players, and making sound tactical decisions during matches (see chapter 10 for more information on coaching during matches). Remember that the focus is not on winning at all costs but on coaching your kids to compete well, do their best, improve their skills, and strive to win within the rules.

6. Help your players become fit and value fitness for a lifetime.

We want young players to become fit so that they can play soccer safely and successfully. We also want them to understand the value of fitness, learn to become fit on their own, and enjoy training. Thus, we ask you not to make them do push-ups or run laps for punishment. Make it fun to get fit for soccer, and make it fun to play the game so that they'll stay fit for a lifetime.

7. Help young people develop character.

Character development includes learning, caring, being honest and respectful, and taking responsibility. These intangible qualities are no less important to teach than the skill of tackling well. We ask you to teach these values to players by demonstrating and encouraging behaviors that express these values at all times. For example, while teaching tackling, stress to young players not only the importance of learning when and where to tackle but also the importance of helping their teammates, playing within the rules, and showing respect for their opponents. Help them understand that they are responsible for winning the individual duel, even though they may not be recognized individually for their efforts.

As you exercise your responsibilities, remember that every player is an individual. You must provide a wholesome environment in which each one has the opportunity to learn how to play the game without fear while having fun and enjoying the overall soccer experience.

Coaching Your Own Child

Coaching can become even more complicated when your child plays on the team you coach. Many coaches are parents, but the two roles should not be confused. As a parent, you are responsible only for yourself and your child, but as a coach you are also responsible for the organization, all the players on the team, and their parents. Because of this additional responsibility, your behavior on the soccer field will be different from your behavior at home, and your son or daughter may not understand why.

COACHING TIP Some parents have found that coaching helps keep their own children involved in soccer. Others find coaching their own child a recipe for disaster because the child resents the switch from nurturing parent to neutral or demanding coach who can't play favorites. Discuss the decision with your child.

For example, imagine the confusion of a young boy who is the center of his parents' attention at home but is barely noticed by his father (who is the coach) in the soccer setting; or consider the mixed signals a young girl receives when her skill is constantly evaluated by her mother, the coach, who otherwise rarely comments on her daughter's activities. You need to explain to your child what your new responsibilities are and how they will affect your relationship when you're coaching. Take the following steps to avoid problems when coaching your own child:

- Ask your child whether she wants you to coach the team.
- Explain why you want to be involved with the team.
- Discuss with your child how your interactions will change when you take on the role of coach at training sessions or matches.
- Limit your coaching behavior to when you are in the coaching role.
- Avoid parenting during training or match situations in order to keep your role clear in your child's mind.
- Reaffirm your love for your child, irrespective of his performance on the soccer field.

Five Tools of an Effective Coach

Have you purchased the traditional coaching tools—things such as disc cones, coaching clothes, soccer shoes, and a water bottle? They'll help you with your coaching, but to be successful you'll need five other tools that you cannot buy. These tools are available only through self-examination and hard work; they're easy to remember with the acronym COACH:

C   Comprehension
O   Outlook
A   Affection
C   Character
H   Humor

Comprehension

Coaching requires that you comprehend the rules and skills of soccer. You must understand the basic elements of the sport. To improve your comprehension of soccer, take the following steps:

- Read about the rules of soccer in chapter 3 of this book.
- Read about the fundamental skills of soccer in chapters 7, 8, and 9.
- Read additional soccer coaching books, including those available from the American Sport Education Program (ASEP).
- Contact youth soccer organizations, including US Youth Soccer (www.usyouthsoccer.org).
- Attend soccer coaching clinics. Check with your state soccer association for dates and locations.
- Talk with more experienced coaches.
- Observe local professional, college, high school, and youth soccer games.
- Watch soccer matches on television.

In addition to having soccer knowledge, you must implement proper training and safety methods so that your players can participate with little risk of injury. Even then, injuries may occur. More often than not, you'll be the first person responding to your players' injuries, so be sure you understand the basic emergency care procedures described in chapter 4. Also, read in that chapter how to handle more serious sport injury situations.

Outlook

This coaching tool refers to your perspective and goals—what you seek as a coach. The most common coaching objectives are to (a) have fun; (b) help players develop their physical, mental, and social skills; and (c) help players strive to play their best consistently. Thus, your outlook involves your priorities, your planning, and your vision for the future. See Assessing Your Priorities to learn more about the priorities you set for yourself as a coach.

ASEP has a motto that will help you keep your outlook in line with the best interests of the kids on your team. It summarizes in four words all you need to remember when establishing your coaching priorities:

> Athletes first, winning second.

This motto recognizes that striving to win is an important, even vital, part of sports. But it emphatically states that no efforts to win should be made at the expense of the players' well-being, development, and enjoyment. Take the following actions to better define your outlook:

- With your coaches, determine your priorities for the season.
- Prepare for situations that challenge your priorities.
- Set goals for yourself and your players that are consistent with your priorities.
- Plan how you and your players can best attain your goals.
- Review your goals frequently to be sure that you are staying on track.

Affection

Another vital tool you need in your coaching kit is a genuine concern for the young people you coach. It requires having a passion for kids, a desire to share with them your enjoyment and knowledge of soccer, and the patience and understanding that allow each player to grow from being involved in sports. You can demonstrate your affection and patience in many ways, including the following:

- Make an effort to get to know each player on your team.
- Treat each player as an individual.
- Empathize with players trying to learn new and difficult skills.
- Treat players as you would like to be treated under similar circumstances.
- Control your emotions.
- Show your enthusiasm for being involved with your team.
- Keep an upbeat tempo and a positive tone in all of your communications.
- Share your passion for soccer.

COACHING TIP   Children won't care what you know until they know that you care.

Assessing Your Priorities

Even though all coaches focus on competition, we want you to focus on *positive* competition. Keep the pursuit of victory in perspective—make decisions that, first, are in the best interests of the players, and second, will help to win the match.

How do you know whether your outlook and priorities are in order? Here's a little test:

1. Which situation would make you proud?
   a. *knowing that each player enjoyed playing soccer*
   b. *seeing that all players improved their soccer skills*
   c. *winning the league championship*
2. Which statement best reflects your thoughts about soccer?
   a. *If it isn't fun, don't do it.*
   b. *Everyone should learn something every day.*
   c. *Soccer isn't fun if you don't win.*
3. How would you like your players to remember you?
   a. *as a coach who created a fun experience*
   b. *as a coach who provided a good base of fundamental skills*
   c. *as a coach who had a winning record*
4. Which would you most like to hear a parent of a player on your team say?
   a. *Mike really had a good time playing soccer this year.*
   b. *Nicole learned some important lessons playing soccer this year.*
   c. *Willie played on the first-place soccer team this year.*
5. Which of the following would be the most rewarding moment of your season?
   a. *having your team want to continue playing, even after training is over*
   b. *seeing one of your players finally master the skill of dribbling*
   c. *winning the league championship*

Look over your answers. If you most often selected *a* responses, then having fun is most important to you. A majority of *b* answers suggests that skill development is what attracts you to coaching. And if *c* was your most frequent response, winning is tops on your list of coaching priorities. If your priorities are in order, your players' well-being will take precedence over your team's win–loss record every time.

Character

The fact that you have decided to coach young soccer players probably means that you think participation in sports is important. But whether or not such participation develops character in your players depends as much on you as it does on the sport itself. How can you help your players build character?

Having good character means modeling appropriate behaviors for sport and life. That means more than just saying the right things—what you say and what you do must match. There is no place in coaching for the "Do as I say, not as I do" philosophy. Challenge, support, encourage, and reward every youngster, and your players will be more likely to accept, even celebrate, their differences. Be in control before, during, and after all training sessions and matches. And don't be afraid to admit it when you're wrong. No one is perfect.

Each member of your coaching staff should consider the following steps to becoming a good role model:

- Take stock of your strengths and weaknesses.
- Build on your strengths.
- Set goals for yourself to improve on those weak areas.
- If you slip up, apologize to your team and to yourself. You'll do better next time.

Humor

Humor is an often overlooked coaching tool. For our purpose, it means having the ability to laugh at yourself and with your players during practices and competition. Nothing helps balance the seriousness of a training session like a chuckle or two, and a sense of humor puts in perspective the many mistakes your players will make. Don't get upset over each miscue or respond negatively to erring players. Allow your players and yourself to enjoy the ups, and don't dwell on the downs. Here are some tips for injecting humor into your practices:

- Make practices fun by including a variety of activities.
- Keep all players involved in matches and training sessions.
- Consider laughter by your players a sign of enjoyment, not of waning discipline.
- Smile!

Communicating
as a Coach

In chapter 1 you learned about the tools you need for coaching: comprehension, outlook, affection, character, and humor. These are essentials for effective coaching; without them, you'd have a difficult time getting started. But none of the tools will work if you don't know how to use them with your players—and doing so requires skillful communication. This chapter examines what communication is and how you can become a more effective communicator.

Coaches often mistakenly believe that communication occurs only when they're instructing players to do something, but verbal commands are only a small part of the communication process. More than half of what you communicate is conveyed nonverbally, so remember this when you are coaching: Actions speak louder than words.

Communication in its simplest form involves two people: a sender and a receiver. The sender transmits the message verbally, through facial expressions, and possibly through body language. Once the message is sent, the receiver must receive it and, optimally, understand it. A receiver who fails to pay attention or listen will miss part, if not all, of the message.

Sending Effective Messages

Young players often have little understanding of the rules and skills of soccer and probably even less confidence in their ability to play the game. They need accurate, understandable, and supportive messages to help them along. That's why your verbal and nonverbal messages count.

Verbal Messages

"Sticks and stones may break my bones, but words will never hurt me" isn't true. Spoken words can have a strong and lasting effect. Coaches' words are particularly influential because youngsters place great importance on what coaches say. Perhaps you, like many former youth athletes, have a difficult time remembering much of anything you were told by your elementary school teachers, but you can still recall several specific things your coaches at that level said to you. Such is the lasting effect of a coach's comments on a player.

Whether you are correcting misbehavior, teaching a player how to pass the ball, or praising a player for good effort, you should consider a number of things when sending a message verbally:

- Be positive and honest.
- State it clearly and simply.
- Say it loud enough, and say it again.
- Be consistent.

Be Positive and Honest

Nothing turns people off like hearing someone nag all the time, and players react similarly to a coach who gripes constantly. Kids particularly need encouragement because they often doubt their abilities to perform in soccer. Look for what your players do well and tell them. But don't cover up poor or incorrect play with rosy words of praise. Kids know all too well when they've erred, and no cheerfully expressed cliche can undo their mistakes. If you fail to acknowledge players' errors, they will think you are a phony.

An effective way to correct a performance error is to first point out the part of the skill that the player performed correctly. Then explain—in a positive manner—the error the player made and show her the correct way to do it. Finish by encouraging the player and emphasizing the correct performance.

Be sure not to follow a positive statement with the word *but*. For example, don't say, "That was good accuracy on your pass, Kelly, but if you follow through with your kick a little more, you'll get more zip on the ball." Such a remark causes many kids to ignore the positive statement and focus on the negative one. Instead, try something like this: "That was good accuracy on your pass, Kelly. And if you follow through with your kick a little more, you'll get more zip on the ball. That was right on target. Way to go." This is an example of the sandwich technique: Start with a positive comment, provide the critique, and finish with a positive comment.

State It Clearly and Simply

Positive and honest messages are good but only if expressed directly in words your players understand. Beating around the bush is ineffective and inefficient. If you ramble, your players will miss the point of your message and probably lose interest. Here are tips for saying things clearly:

- Organize your thoughts before speaking to your players.
- Know your subject as completely as possible.
- Explain things thoroughly, but don't bore your players with long-winded monologues.
- Use language your players can understand, and be consistent in your terminology. However, avoid trying to be hip by using their age group's slang.

COACHING TIP With the U6 and U8 age groups, give your instructions, comments, or questions in 30 seconds or less. With the U10 and U12 age groups, give your instructions, comments, or questions in 45 seconds or less. With the U14 age group, give your instructions, comments, or questions in 1 minute or less.

Say It Loud Enough, and Say It Again

Talk to your team in a voice that all members can hear. A crisp, vigorous voice commands attention and respect; garbled and weak speech is tuned out. It's OK, and in fact appropriate, to soften your voice when speaking to a player individually about a personal problem. But most of the time your messages will be for all your players to hear, so make sure they can. An enthusiastic voice also motivates players and tells them you enjoy being their coach. A word of caution, however: Avoid dominating the setting with a booming voice that distracts attention from players' performances. When a player enters into a mental state of flow, it can be a powerful learning environment, in which case interrupting a player's rhythm can do more harm than good.

Sometimes what you say, even if you state it loudly and clearly, won't sink in the first time. This may be particularly true when young players hear words they don't understand. To avoid boring repetition and still get your message across, say the same thing in a slightly different way. For instance, you might first tell your players, "Mark your opponents tighter!" If they don't appear to understand, you might say, "When your opponents are in shooting range, you can't give them the chance to shoot or pass the ball forward." The second form of the message may get through to players who missed it the first time around.

COACHING TIP Remember, terms that you are familiar with and understand may be completely foreign to your players, especially the beginners. Use a vocabulary appropriate for the age group. A 6-year-old most likely will not comprehend some words that a 12-year-old will understand.

Be Consistent

People often say things in ways that imply a different message. For example, a touch of sarcasm added to the words "Way to go!" sends an entirely different message than the words themselves suggest. Avoid sending mixed messages. Keep the tone of your voice consistent with the words you use. Don't say something one day and contradict it the next; players will get their wires crossed.

Keep your terminology consistent. Many soccer terms describe the same or a similar skill. One coach may use the term *halfback* to describe a position in the middle of the team, whereas another coach may call the same position *midfielder*. Both are correct. To be consistent as a staff, however, agree on all terms before the start of the season, and then stay with them.

Nonverbal Messages

Just as you must be consistent in the tone of voice and words you use, you must also keep your verbal and nonverbal messages consistent. An extreme example of failing to do so would be shaking your head, indicating disapproval, and at the same time telling a player, "Nice try." Which is the player to believe, your gesture or your words?

You can send messages nonverbally in several ways. Facial expressions and body language are just two of the more obvious forms of nonverbal signals that can help you when you coach. Keep in mind that a coach needs to be a teacher first, and any action that detracts from the message you are trying to convey should be avoided.

Facial Expressions

The look on a person's face is the quickest clue to what he thinks or feels. Your players know this, so they will study your face, looking for a sign that will tell them more than the words you say. Don't try to fool them by putting on a happy or blank mask. They'll see through it, and you'll lose credibility.

Serious, stone-faced expressions provide no cues to kids who want to know how they are performing. When faced with such, kids will just assume you're unhappy or disinterested. Don't be afraid to smile. A smile from a coach can give a great boost to an unsure player. Plus, a smile lets your players know that you are happy coaching them. But don't overdo it, or they won't be able to tell when you are genuinely pleased by something they've done and when you are just putting on a smiling face.

Body Language

What would your players think you were feeling if you came to training slouched over, with your head down and shoulders slumped? That you were tired, bored, or unhappy? What would they think you were feeling if you watched them during a match with your hands on your hips, your jaws clenched, and your face reddened? Would they get the impression that you were upset with them, disgusted at a referee, or mad at a fan? Probably some or all of these things would enter your players' minds. None of them are impressions you want your players to have of you. That's why you should carry yourself in a pleasant, confident, and vigorous manner.

COACHING TIP A good-humored, energetic posture not only projects happiness with your coaching role but also provides a good example for your young players, who may model your behavior. Whereas prepubescent children do pick up on the coach's mannerisms, pubescent children are particularly aware of the coach's actions. Be prepared at all times to walk the talk.

Physical contact can also be an essential use of body language. A handshake, a pat on the head, an arm around the shoulder, and even a big hug are effective ways to show approval, concern, affection, and joy to your players. Youngsters are especially in need of this type of nonverbal message. Keep within the obvious moral and legal limits, of course, but don't be reluctant to touch your players, sending a message that can be expressed only by such contact.

Improving Your Receiving Skills

Now, let's examine the other half of the communication process: receiving messages. Too often, good senders are poor receivers of messages. As a coach of young players, you must be able to fulfill both roles effectively.

The requirements for receiving messages are quite simple, but some people find receiving skills less satisfying than sending skills; therefore, they do not work at them. People seem to enjoy hearing themselves talk more than they enjoy hearing others talk. But if you learn the keys of receiving messages and make a strong effort to use them with your players, you'll be surprised by what you've been missing.

Pay Attention

First, you must pay attention—you must want to hear what others have to communicate to you. That's not always easy when you're busy coaching and have many things competing for your attention. But in one-on-one or team meetings with players, you must focus on what they are telling you, both verbally and nonverbally. You'll be amazed at the little signals you pick up. Focused attention not only helps you catch every word your players say but also helps you take in your players' moods and physical states. In addition, you'll get an idea of your players' feelings toward you and others on the team. It is especially important to listen more than talk during a match. As a player-centered sport, soccer requires players to talk to each other, and you need to hear what they are saying.

> **COACHING TIP** You'll see training sessions during which the coach is talking all the time. The players want to continue playing, but the coach is rambling on. Hundreds of thousands of youth soccer coaches across America do the same thing during matches. When the coach takes center stage this way, it takes the game away from the players. But the game is all about the players, and the players are the game.

Listen Carefully

Perhaps more than anything else, how we receive messages from others demonstrates how much we care for the sender and for what that person has to tell us. If you have little regard for your players or for what they have to say, it will show in how you attend to them. Check yourself. Do you find your mind wandering to what you are going to do after practice while one of your players is talking to you? Do you frequently have to ask your players, "What did you say?" If so, you need to work on the receiving mechanics of attending and listening. If you find that you're missing the messages your players send, the most critical question you should ask yourself is this: Do I care?

If you do care, then you'll want your players' input. The degree of input will depend on their age. As an example, too many coaches carry on a monologue at halftime, and the players never have a say in the second-half game plan. Yet they are the ones who must execute it. Instead, the halftime talk should be a dialogue between the coach and players on what to do for the second half. As to age appropriateness, that talk with the U6 age group will be one question, one comment, and then "Let's play." With the U14 age group, the talk should be more detailed. The point is to give ownership of the game to the players, so you must involve them in the team decision-making process. Remember that once the match begins, it is completely up to the players.

Providing Feedback

So far we've discussed the sending and receiving of messages separately. But we all know that senders and receivers switch roles several times during an interaction. One person initiates communication by sending a message to another person, the receiver. The receiver then becomes the sender by responding to the person who sent the initial message. These verbal and nonverbal responses are called feedback.

Your players will look to you for feedback all the time. They will want to know how you think they are performing, what you think of their ideas, and whether their efforts please you. You can respond in many different ways, and how you respond will strongly affect your players. They will react most favorably to positive feedback.

Praising players when they have performed or behaved well is an effective way of encouraging them to repeat (or try to repeat) that behavior. And positive feedback for effort is an especially effective way to motivate youngsters to work on difficult skills. Rather than shouting at players who have made mistakes and giving them negative feedback, try offering positive feedback by letting them know what they did correctly and how they can improve. Sometimes just the way you word feedback can make it more encouraging than not. For example, instead of saying, "Don't shoot the ball that way," you might say, "Shoot the ball this way." Then your players will focus on what to do instead of what not to do. Be careful, though, to not overpraise. Be a coach, not a cheerleader.

COACHING TIP Here are a dozen ways to commend your athletes: 1. I think you've got it now. 2. Outstanding! 3. I'm proud of the way you worked today. 4. Now you've got it! 5. Tremendous! 6. Hurray for you! 7. You certainly did well today. 8. Perfect. 9. You've got your brain in gear today. 10. Good! 11. Now you have the hang of it. 12. Bingo!

Positive feedback can be verbal or nonverbal. Telling young players that they have performed well, especially in front of teammates, is a great way to boost their confidence. And a pat on the back or a handshake communicates that you recognize a player's performance.

Communicating With Others

Coaching involves not only sending and receiving messages and providing proper feedback to players but also interacting with members of the staff, parents, fans, officials, and opposing coaches. If you don't communicate effectively with these groups, your coaching career will be unpleasant and short lived. Try the following suggestions for communicating with these groups.

Coaching Staff

Before you hold your first practice, the coaching staff must meet and discuss the roles and responsibilities that each coach will undertake during the year. Staff responsibilities can be divided into head coach, assistant coaches, and team manager, depending on the number of volunteers. Some clubs may also have a goalkeeper coach. The head coach has the final responsibility for all phases of the game, but the assistant coaches should take on as much responsibility in their roles as possible.

Before training sessions start, the coaching staff must also discuss and agree on terminology, plans for training, organization on match day, and methods of communicating during training sessions and matches. The coaches on your staff must present a united front; they must all take a similar approach to coaching, interacting with players and parents, and interacting with one another. Conduct discussions of disagreements away from the playing field so that each coach can have a say and the staff can come to an agreement.

Parents

A player's parents need to be assured that their child is under the direction of a coach who is both knowledgeable about the sport and concerned about each youngster's well-being. You can put their worries to rest by holding a preseason orientation meeting for parents, in which you describe your background and your approach to coaching (see Preseason Meeting Topics).

If parents contact you with a concern during the season, listen to them closely, and try to offer positive responses. If you need to communicate with parents, catch them after training, give them a phone call, or send a note through e-mail or the U.S. mail. Messages sent to parents through players are too often lost, misinterpreted, or forgotten. Parents may also connect with US Youth Soccer's parent assistance program (which provides parents with information on how to interact with their child in soccer, how to communicate with their child's coach, and so on) at www.usyouthsoccer.org/parents.

Preseason Meeting Topics

1. Share your philosophy of coaching.
2. Outline paperwork that is needed for the club:
   - Copy of player's birth certificate
   - Completed player's application and payment record
   - Informed consent form (page 191)
   - Emergency information card (page 193)
3. Review the inherent risks of soccer and other safety issues, and go over your emergency action plan.
4. Inform parents of uniform and equipment costs and needs.
5. Review the season training schedule including date, location, and time of each training session.
6. Discuss nutrition, hydration, and rest for players.
7. Explain goals for the team.
8. Cover methods of communication: e-mail list, emergency phone numbers, interactive Web site, and so on.
9. Discuss ways that parents can help with the team.
10. Discuss standards of conduct for coaches, players, and parents.
11. Provide time for questions and answers.

Fans

The stands probably won't be overflowing at your matches, which means you'll more easily hear the few fans who criticize your coaching. When you hear something negative about the job you're doing, don't respond. Keep calm, consider whether the message has any value, and if not, forget it. Acknowledging critical, unwarranted comments from a fan during a match will only encourage others to voice their opinions. So put away your rabbit ears and communicate to fans, through your actions, that you are a confident, competent coach.

Prepare your players, too, for fan criticism. Tell them they should listen to you, not the spectators. If you notice that one of your players is rattled by a fan's comment, reassure the player that your evaluation is more objective and favorable—and it's the one that counts.

Referees

How you communicate with referees will have a great influence on the way your players behave toward them; therefore, you must set a good example. Greet referees with a handshake, an introduction, and perhaps casual conversation about the upcoming match. Indicate your respect for them before, during, and after the match. Don't make nasty remarks, shout, or use disrespectful body gestures. Your players will see you do these things, and they'll get the idea that such behavior is appropriate. Plus, if the referee hears or sees you, the communication between the two of you will break down.

Opposing Coaches

Make an effort to visit with the coach of the opposing team before the match. During the match, don't get into a personal feud with the opposing coach. Remember—it's the kids, not the coaches, who are competing. And by getting along well with the opposing coach, you'll show your players that competition involves cooperation.

Understanding Rules and Equipment

Soccer is a simple game played by teams divided into 3 to 11 players per side. It is governed by rules that are modified for the age group you are coaching. This introduction to the basic rules of soccer won't cover every rule of the game but will give you the fundamentals for working with players who are 6 to 14 years old. This chapter covers field markings, ball and goal sizes, and equipment. It also describes player positions, match procedures, and scoring; reviews the rules of play; and gives an overview of officiating and common officiating signals.

Age Modifications for Soccer

Before we begin, however, familiarize yourself with the concept of adjusting the size of the field, goal, and ball; the number of players on the field; and the duration of the game for various age groups to accommodate players' developmental and skill levels. These adjustments are as follows:

For more detailed information on rule modifications, please refer to the US Youth Soccer playing recommendations for each specific age group at www.usyouthsoccer.org.

	U6	U8	U10	U12	U14
Players on team	**Single field method:** 4-6 **Dual field method:** 8-10	**Single field method:** 6-8 **Dual field method:** 10-12	**Single field method:** 9-11 **Dual field method:** 14-16	11-13	11-18
Ball size	3	3	4	4	5
Goal size	6 × 18 ft or smaller	6 × 18 ft or smaller	6 × 18 ft	6 × 18 ft	8 × 24 ft
Field size	25 × 20 yd	35 × 25 yd	55 × 40 yd	80 × 50 yd	100 × 65 yd
Players on field	3 per team	4 per team	6 per team	8 per team	11 per team
Length of game	4 × 8 min	4 × 12 min	2 × 25 min	2 × 30 min	2 × 35 min

RULES

Field

The Laws of the Game allow for the length and width of the field to vary within set yardages, for age groups up to 16 and every level of competition. The field markings within the boundary lines must be the same for every level of competition, as shown in figure 3.1, but they are modified for the specific age groups. Some field markings you see on the field of play for teenage and adult players will not be on the field for the younger players. For example, on the U6 and U8 fields of play, the penalty area is not marked on the field as it is for the U10 and older age groups. The following markings define all fields (for additional soccer definitions, please refer to the glossary starting on page 195).

- *Goal line:* The end line of the field, on which the goal sits. The goal line runs from corner to corner.
- *Touchline:* The sideline that runs the length of the field of play from corner to corner.
- *Corner arc:* The four 1-yard arcs, one in each corner of the field of play, from which players take corner kicks.
- *Goal area:* The small box immediately in front of the goal from which players take goal kicks.
- *Penalty kick spot:* The spot inside the penalty area from which players take penalty kicks.
- *Penalty area:* The large box in front of the goal. Fouls committed by the defending team that normally result in a direct free kick will result in a penalty kick when the foul is committed inside their penalty area. This is the area in which the goalkeeper may use his hands.

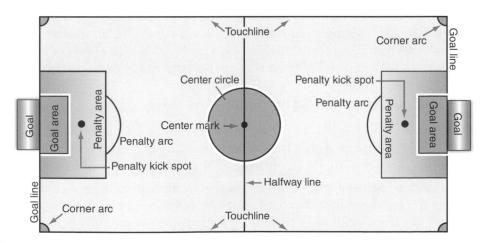

FIGURE 3.1 Soccer field markings.

- *Halfway line:* The line that runs across the field of play from touchline to touchline and divides the field in half.
- *Center circle:* The circle in the center of the field surrounding the center mark, outside of which the defending team must remain until the ball is put into play at a kickoff.
- *Center mark:* The spot on the halfway line where the ball is placed for a kickoff.

Player Equipment

Soccer players need very little equipment to play the game. These items include multistudded soccer shoes (recommended for outdoor play but not required), loose-fitting clothing appropriate for the weather (goalkeepers wear a jersey in a different color), and shin guards worn under knee-length socks to protect players' legs. Gloves for goalkeepers have always been optional equipment, used predominantly to grip the ball better rather than to protect the hands. In cold weather, gloves can also help keep goalkeepers' hands warm and flexible for catching the ball.

Make sure that players on your team are outfitted properly and that the equipment they obtain meets acceptable standards. Advise players and their parents about how players' shoes should fit and how players should break shoes in when they are new. Occasionally inspect shin guards to be sure they are in good condition.

Player Positions

Give your young players a chance to play a variety of positions. By playing different positions, they'll have a better all-around playing experience and will stay more interested in the sport. Furthermore, they'll have a better understanding of the many technical and tactical skills used in the game. The players will also better appreciate the efforts of their teammates who play positions they themselves find difficult.

Following are descriptions of the positions for soccer.

- *Forward:* Forwards play closer to the other team's goal and shoot the ball more than other players. The forwards that play nearest the touchlines are called wingers; those in the middle of the field are referred to as strikers.
- *Midfielder:* Midfielders are all-purpose players who take shots and try to win the ball from the other team. They are transition players, helping move the ball from defense to offense. Their position is named appropriately since they play between forwards and defenders on the field.
- *Defender:* Defenders play near their own team's goal and try to prevent the other team from shooting the ball. They also receive the ball from the goalkeeper and move the ball up the field to begin the attack.

- *Goalkeeper:* A goalkeeper plays in front of the goal and tries to prevent the ball from getting into the goal. The goalkeeper is the only player allowed to use the hands to block shots and to initiate the attack from within the team's penalty area.

Soccer uses different alignments for different age groups (see table 3.1). In all cases, the numbers that describe team formation—as shown in the formation used column of table 3.1—go from the back to the front, and the goalkeeper is assumed (except for the U6 and U8 age groups, for which no goalkeepers are used). For example, in the U14 age group, which uses 11 players on the field per team, a formation could be 4-3-3. These numbers mean four defenders, three midfielders, and three forwards. Please note, however, that these are not the only formations that can work with your players. You should choose a team formation that best executes the principles of play and that makes it easy for your players to support one another on offense and defense.

For the U6 age group there is no team formation. Coaches of the U6 age group should not be dismayed if players tend to congregate around the ball simultaneously, because this is the nature of the age group. For the U8 age group, however, two formations—the box or the diamond—can be used. The diamond consists of four players assuming a diamondlike shape, with one player in back, two on the sides, and one in front. The box consists of two players in back and two players in front. In either case, remember that U8 players will have only slightly more understanding of group shape than the U6 age group, so don't be dismayed if they tend to stray from these formations and bunch around the ball.

The U10 through U14 age groups use more complex formations. For the U10 age group, you can use two basic formations—three defenders and two forwards, or the reverse. US Youth Soccer recommends the 3-2 formation. For the U12 age group, three basic formations, a 3-2-2, a 3-3-1, or a 2-3-2, can be used. At this level, if the coach and team wish to forgo a midfield line, they can use a 4-3 formation. US Youth Soccer recommends the formation with two defenders, three midfielders, and two forwards. For the U14 age group, you can use two basic formations—a 4-3-3 or a 3-4-3. US Youth Soccer recommends the formation with three defenders, four midfielders, and three forwards.

TABLE 3.1 Soccer Formations for Age Groups

Age group	Players on field	Formation used
U6	3v3	N/A
U8	4v4	Box or diamond
U10	6v6	3-2
U12	8v8	2-3-2
U14	11v11	3-4-3

Rules of Play

Soccer rules are designed to make the match run smoothly and safely and to prevent either team from gaining an unfair advantage. Following is an overview of some of the basic rules in soccer.

Starting the Match

Soccer matches begin with one team, chosen by a coin toss, kicking the ball from the center mark. The opposing team's players are not allowed within the center circle during the kickoff. Players on both teams must be on their half of the field during the kickoff, and the kicked ball must roll forward before another player may touch it.

The same procedures are followed after a goal is scored. In this situation, the team that was scored on restarts the match by kicking off from the center mark, and the team that scored stands outside of the center circle in its half of the field.

Restarting the Game

Several situations may cause a referee to stop play during a match, and play must restart accordingly (depending on the reason for stopping play). Play is also stopped when a ball goes out of bounds beyond the goal line or along the touchline.

When an attacking team kicks the ball out of bounds beyond the goal line, as in a missed shot, the opposing team is awarded a free kick called a goal kick. The defending team makes this kick from anywhere inside the goal area. The majority of the time, the goal kick should be played upfield and out toward the touchlines, as shown in figure 3.2. The players on the team that kicked the ball out of bounds must stay outside the penalty area until the ball clears the penalty area.

If a team kicks the ball beyond its own goal line, the other team is awarded a corner kick from the corner arc on the side of the field where the ball went out. During the kick, defending players must be at least 10 yards, or a distance equivalent to the diameter of the center circle, from the player kicking the ball. The kicker's teammates may position themselves anywhere they choose. Corner kicks are most commonly made into three areas—the near post, the far post, and the penalty spot—as shown in figure 3.3.

COACHING TIP Many U6 and U8 players do not yet have the eye–hand coordination to execute a throw-in, so for these age groups a kick-in is used to replace the throw-in. For a kick-in, the ball is on the ground and stationary so that U6 and U8 players have a better chance of striking it correctly.

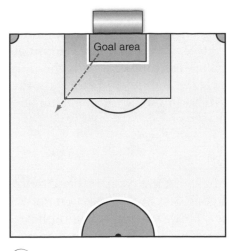

FIGURE 3.2   Goal kick location.

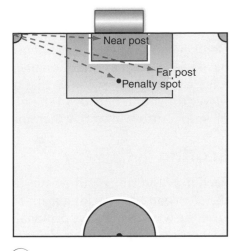

FIGURE 3.3   Corner kick locations.

When a player kicks the ball out of bounds along the touchline, the match is restarted with a throw-in at the spot where the ball went out (see figure 3.4). The team that last touched the ball loses possession, and the other team gets to throw in the ball. The player putting the ball back into play must use both hands to throw the ball and keep both feet on the ground. The throwing motion should begin from behind the head and maintain a continuous forward thrust until the ball is released in front of the head. The throw-in should be put into play quickly, thrown to the feet of a teammate who is not being marked.

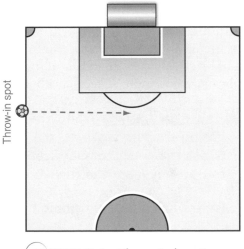

FIGURE 3.4   Throw-in location.

Play is also stopped for no-penalty situations such as those mentioned in Soccer No-Nos on page 29. In these cases, play is restarted with a drop ball.

Goalkeeping

A goalkeeper, whose main responsibility is to stop shots on goal, is the last line of defense and the first line of attack. In youth soccer, as previously noted in this chapter, goalkeepers are not introduced until the U10 age group.

Goalkeepers may use their hands within their penalty area. They may also use their hands to collect a ball that a teammate has headed to them deliberately. Goalkeepers, however, may not use their hands to collect a ball that a teammate has kicked to them intentionally. When a goalkeeper catches a ball, she must release it within 6 seconds. She may not touch the ball again before another player touches it outside of the penalty area. In addition, goalkeepers may not pick up a throw-in from a teammate.

Scoring

Each time the entire ball crosses the goal line between the goalposts and below the crossbar, the attacking team is awarded a goal. Scoring a goal is one of the tangible ways to measure personal performance. However, don't overemphasize goal scoring in assessing a player's contribution. Give equal attention to players who make assists, tackles, interceptions, or saves and who demonstrate leadership, sporting behavior, and effort.

Rule Infractions

Although no soccer team will perform foul free, teach your players to avoid recurring fouls. For example, if an infraction occurs in training, stop the play and briefly discuss the result of the foul. By instilling this discipline, you'll help players enjoy more success, both as individuals and as a team.

> **COACHING TIP** When the coach enforces the Laws of the Game during training sessions, the players learn the rules and have a chance to ask the coach for clarification. This is the best way for young players to not only learn the rules but also find out how to play by the rules.

Following are several common infractions that soccer players commit.

Fouls

The referee calls a foul when one player charges, pushes, trips or attempts to trip, kicks or attempts to kick, spits at, or holds an opposing player or tackles an opponent before the ball. A handball foul is called when a player intentionally touches the ball with his hand or arm.

Players who keep fouling intentionally or playing dangerously are warned once by the referee. Persistent infractions may result in a yellow card caution (a warning from the official). The next time the player intentionally fouls or plays dangerously, the referee gives him a red card and ejects him from the match. Referees can also eject a player without warning if they rule a behavior unacceptable.

Free Kicks

Fouls usually result in either a direct or an indirect free kick, depending on the type of foul (see table 3.2). Players may strike direct free kicks right to the goal, whereas indirect free kicks must touch a player other than the original kicker before a goal can be scored. Opponents must be at least 10 yards (or a distance equivalent to the diameter of the center circle) away from the ball during a free kick. A free kick awarded within a defending team's own goal area may be taken from any point within the goal area. An indirect free kick awarded to the attacking team within the opponent's goal area is taken from the line at the top of the goal area nearest to the point of the infraction. The referee will signal which type of free kick has been awarded.

TABLE 3.2 Free Kick Fouls

Direct kick	Indirect kick
Handball	Playing dangerously
Kicking or attempting to kick an opponent	Obstruction
Striking or attempting to strike an opponent	Goalkeeper taking more than 6 sec to release the ball
Tripping or attempting to trip an opponent	Offside
Holding an opponent	Goalkeeper touching the ball with his hands after it has been released from his possession and has not yet been touched by a second player
Pushing an opponent	
Jumping at an opponent	Goalkeeper catching the ball on a throw-in from a teammate or after it has been kicked to her by a teammate
Charging at an opponent	
Spitting at an opponent	

Penalty Kicks

Penalty kicks are awarded to the attacking team if a defending player commits a direct kick foul inside the penalty area. A penalty kick is a free shot at the goal by an individual attacker, with only the goalkeeper defending against the shot. Penalty kicks are taken from the penalty kick spot in front of the center of the goal, as shown in figure 3.1 on page 21. This distance is 10 yards for U12. For older participants, the distance is 12 yards. The goalkeeper may not leave the goal line until after the ball is kicked.

Offside

A player is in an offside position when he is closer to the opponent's goal than at least two defending players when the ball is passed forward. As you can see in figure 3.5, player 2 is offside. The offside rule prevents attacking players from simply waiting at the goalmouth for an easy shot, but it does not apply to throw-ins, corner kicks, or instances in which players are in their own half of the field. When a player is offside, the opposing team receives an indirect free kick at the point of the infraction.

Also, note that a player is not called offside merely for being in an offside position. The player must be participating in the play to be ruled offside. For example, if play is occurring on one side of the field, and a player on the other side of the field is in an offside position but is not involved in the play going on across the field (i.e., a teammate is not passing or attempting to pass to her), then that player won't be ruled offside. As you can see in figure 3.6, player 2 is not participating in the play and therefore not in violation of the offside rule.

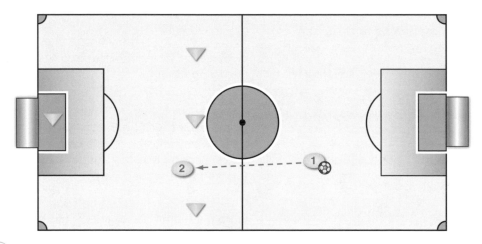

FIGURE 3.5   Offside foul.

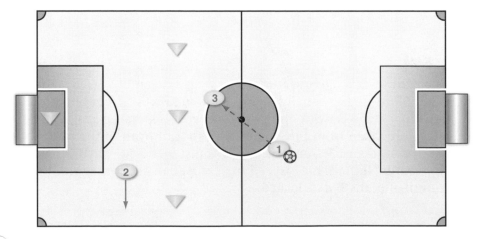

FIGURE 3.6   Offside—no call.

Soccer No-Nos

It is inevitable that your players will violate minor rules during training sessions and matches now and then. But make clear to your players that some actions are considered bad sporting behavior and may result in a verbal warning or an ejection, depending on the severity or frequency of the infraction. These actions are the following:

- Removing your jersey during a goal celebration
- Feigning an injury or pretending to have been fouled
- Deliberately and blatantly handling the ball to keep an opponent from gaining possession
- Holding an opponent to prevent his gaining possession of the ball or taking up an advantageous position
- Delaying the game
- Excessive or time-wasting goal celebrating
- Making gestures that are provocative, derisory, or inflammatory
- Refusing to leave the field after the match has been stopped to deal with your injury

Officiating

Soccer referees enforce the rules. Their authority over a match begins at least 30 minutes before the start of play and finishes at least 30 minutes after it has ended. In youth soccer, there are typically three officials—a referee and two assistant referees—overseeing the game. For the U6 and U8 age groups there is often only one referee, and in many leagues even the coaches officiate. In the U10 age group, it is common for one certified referee to officiate the game because of the shortage of referees. It is also common for youngsters, some as young as 12 years old, to be the referees. Any official, however, has many responsibilities during a match, including effectively communicating the calls to other members of the referee crew and to the players, coaches, and spectators. See figure 3.7, *a* through *h*, on page 30 for common officiating signals.

In addition, if you have a concern about how referees are officiating a match, address the referees respectfully. Do so immediately if at any time you believe the officiating jeopardizes the safety of your players.

FIGURE 3.7 Officiating signals for (a) goal (points to center of field for kickoff), (b) offside or indirect free kick, (c) caution (yellow card) or ejection (red card), (d) penalty kick (points to penalty spot), (e) advantage or play on, (f) goal kick (points to goal area), (g) corner kick (points to corner arc), and (h) direct free kick.

Providing
for Players' Safety

4

SAFETY

One of your players breaks free down the field, dribbling the ball. Suddenly a defender catches up with, and accidentally trips, the goal-bound player. You notice that your player is not getting up from the ground and seems to be in pain. What do you do?

No coach wants to see players get hurt. But injury remains a reality of sports participation; consequently, you must be prepared to provide first aid when injuries occur and to protect yourself against unjustified lawsuits. Fortunately, coaches can institute many preventive measures to reduce the risks. In this chapter we describe steps you can take to prevent injuries, first aid and emergency responses you can carry out when injuries occur, and legal responsibilities you have as a coach.

Game Plan for Safety

You can't prevent all injuries from happening, but you can take preventive measures that give your players the best possible chance for injury-free participation. In creating the safest possible environment for your players, you can make preparations in these areas:

- Preseason physical examination
- Physical conditioning
- Equipment and facilities inspection
- Player matchups and inherent risks
- Proper supervision and record keeping
- Environmental conditions

Preseason Physical Examination

We recommend that your players have a physical examination before participating in soccer. The exam should address the most likely areas of medical concern and identify youngsters at high risk. We also suggest that you have players' parents or guardians sign a participation agreement form (this will be discussed in more detail later in this chapter) and an informed consent form to allow their children to be treated in case of an emergency. For a sample informed consent form, see page 191 of the appendix.

Physical Conditioning

Players need to be fit or get fit to play the game at the level expected. They must have adequate cardiorespiratory and muscular fitness.

Cardiorespiratory fitness involves the body's ability to use oxygen and fuel efficiently to power muscle contractions. As players get fitter, their bodies are able to more efficiently deliver oxygen to fuel muscles and carry off carbon dioxides and other wastes. Soccer requires lots of running and exertion; most players will move nearly continuously and make short bursts throughout a match. Youngsters who aren't as fit as their peers often overextend in trying to keep up, which can result in light-headedness, nausea, fatigue, and potential injury.

Try to remember that the players' goals are to participate, learn, and have fun. Therefore, you must keep your players active, attentive, and involved with every phase of training. If you do, they will attain higher levels of cardiorespiratory fitness as the season progresses simply by taking part in training. However, watch closely for signs of low cardiorespiratory fitness; don't let your players do much until they're fit. You might privately counsel youngsters who appear overly winded, suggesting that they train under proper supervision outside of training sessions to increase their fitness.

Muscular fitness encompasses strength, muscular endurance, power, speed, and flexibility. This type of fitness is affected by physical maturity as well as by strength training and other types of training. Your players will likely exhibit a relatively wide range of muscular fitness. Those who have greater muscular fitness will be able to run faster and perform more consistently. They will also sustain fewer muscular injuries, and any injuries that do occur will tend to be minor. And in case of injury, recovery is faster in those with higher levels of muscular fitness.

COACHING TIP Children aged 5 to 8 will play all out, with little or no sense of pace, and consequently will fatigue quickly. They will stop activity to rest, and when they resume, they will go flat out again. Preadolescent children aged 5 to 15 will overheat sooner than an adult, so pay close attention to water breaks and to the climate in which training sessions and matches are taking place.

Two other components of fitness and injury prevention are the warm-up and the cool-down. Although young bodies are generally very limber, they can become tight through inactivity. The warm-up should address each muscle group and elevate the heart rate in preparation for strenuous activity. Players should warm up for 5 to 10 minutes using a combination of light, dynamic movement and stretching. As training winds down, slow the players' heart rates with an easy jog or walk. Then have players stretch for 5 minutes to help prevent tight muscles before the next training session or match.

Equipment and Facilities Inspection

Another way to prevent injuries is to check the quality and fit of uniforms, training attire, and protective equipment that your players use. Ensure that all players have adequate shin guards and that they wear them.

Remember also to regularly examine the field on which your players train and play. Remove hazards, report conditions you cannot remedy, and request maintenance as necessary. If unsafe conditions exist, either make adaptations to prevent risk to your players' safety or stop the training session or match until safe conditions have been restored. Refer to the facilities and equipment checklist on page 190 of the appendix to guide you in verifying that facilities are safe.

Player Matchups and Inherent Risks

We recommend that you group teams in two-year age increments if possible. You'll encounter fewer mismatches in physical maturation with narrow age ranges. Even so, two 12-year-old boys might differ greatly in weight, a foot in height, and one to three years in emotional and intellectual maturity. Such variation presents dangers for the less mature. Closely supervise activities so that the more mature do not put the less mature at undue risk.

COACHING TIP Coed teams are perfectly acceptable up until puberty (generally the U12 age group). In the U6 and U8 age groups there are few differences between females and males in height and weight.

Although proper matching of age groups helps protect you from certain liability concerns, you must also warn players of the inherent risks involved in playing soccer because failure to warn is one of the most successful arguments in lawsuits against coaches. Please note that although soccer is not a collision sport, it is a contact sport and injuries are possible. Thoroughly explain the inherent risks of soccer, and make sure each player knows, understands, and appreciates the risks. Some of these intrinsic risks are outlined in chapter 1; learn more about them in this chapter and by talking with your league administrators.

The preseason orientation meeting for parents is a good opportunity to explain the risks of the sport to both parents and players. It is also a good occasion on which to have both the players and their parents sign a waiver releasing you from liability should an injury occur. You should work with your league when creating these forms or waivers, and legal counsel should review them before presentation. These documents do not relieve you of responsibility for your players' well-being, but lawyers recommend them, and they may help you in the event of a lawsuit.

Proper Supervision and Record Keeping

To ensure players' safety, you must provide both general supervision and specific supervision. General supervision means you are in the area of activity so you can see and hear what is happening. You should be

- on the field and in position to supervise the players even before the formal training begins;
- immediately accessible to, and able to oversee, the entire activity;
- alert to conditions that may be dangerous to players and ready to take action to protect players;
- able to react immediately and appropriately to emergencies; and
- present on the field until the last player has been picked up after the training session or match.

Specific supervision is the direct supervision of an activity at training. For example, you should provide specific supervision when you teach new skills and continue it until your players understand the requirements of the activity, the risks involved, and their own ability to perform in light of these risks. You must also provide specific supervision when you notice players breaking rules or see a change in the condition of your players. As a general rule, the more dangerous the activity, the more specific the supervision required. This principle suggests that younger and less experienced players require more specific supervision.

COACHING TIP Although 6-year-olds do indeed need a good bit of supervision during training sessions and matches, they do not generate the force or velocity that teenage players do in respect to impact injuries. They bump into one another, which may cause tears to appear, but it is less likely that a serious injury has occurred. You must attentively supervise all activity, of all age groups, at all training sessions and matches.

As part of your supervisory duties, you are expected to foresee potentially dangerous situations and to help prevent them. This responsibility requires that you know soccer well, especially the rules that are intended to provide for safety. For example, serious injury and possibly death can occur if a goal topples over onto a player, so prohibit dangerous horseplay, and hold training sessions only under safe weather conditions. Such specific supervisory activities, applied consistently, will make the play environment safer for your players and will help protect you from liability if a mishap occurs.

For further protection, keep records of your season plans, practice plans, and players' injuries. Season and practice plans come in handy when you need evidence that you have taught players certain skills, and accurate, detailed injury report forms offer protection against unfounded lawsuits. Ask for these forms from your sponsoring organization (see the Injury Report Form on page 192 of the appendix), and hold onto these records for several years so that a so-called old soccer injury of a former player doesn't come back to haunt you.

Environmental Conditions

Most health problems that environmental factors cause are related to excessive heat or cold, but you should also consider other environmental factors such as severe weather and air pollution. A little thought about the potential problems and a little effort to ensure adequate protection for your players will prevent most serious emergencies related to environmental conditions.

COACHING TIP Encourage players to drink plenty of water before, during, and after training. Water makes up 45 to 65 percent of a young-ster's body weight, and losing even a small amount of water can cause severe consequences in the body's systems. It doesn't have to be hot and humid for players to become dehydrated, nor is thirst an accurate indicator. In fact, by the time players are aware of their thirst, they are long overdue for a drink.

Heat

On hot, humid days the body has difficulty cooling itself. Because the air is already saturated with water vapor (humidity), sweat doesn't evaporate as easily. Therefore, body sweat is a less effective cooling agent, and the body retains extra heat. Hot, humid environments put players at risk of heat exhaustion and heat-stroke (see more on these in Serious Injuries on pages 43-47). And if *you* think it's hot or humid, it's worse for the kids, not only because they're more active but also because kids under the age of 12 have more difficulty regulating their body temperature than do adults. To provide for players' safety in hot or humid conditions, take the following preventive measures.

- Monitor weather conditions, and adjust training sessions accordingly. Table 4.1 shows the specific air temperatures and humidity percentages that can be hazardous.
- Acclimatize players to exercising in high heat and humidity. Players can adjust to high heat and humidity in 7 to 10 days. During this period, hold practices at low to moderate levels of activity, and give the players fluid breaks every 20 minutes or less.
- Switch to light clothing. Players should wear shorts and white T-shirts.
- Identify and monitor players who are prone to heat illness. Players who are overweight, heavily muscled, or out of shape and players who work excessively hard or have experienced previous heat illness are more prone

TABLE 4.1 Warm-Weather Precautions

Temperature (°F)	Humidity	Precautions
80-90	<70%	Monitoring of athletes prone to heat illness
	≥70%	5 min rest after 30 min of practice
90-100	<70%	5 min rest after 30 min of practice
	≥70%	Short practices in eve-ning or early morning

to getting heat illness. Closely monitor these children, and give them fluid breaks every 15 to 20 minutes, or even more frequently for the U6 age group.

- Make sure players replace fluids lost through sweat. Encourage players to drink 17 to 20 ounces of fluid 2 to 3 hours before training sessions or matches and 7 to 10 ounces every 20 minutes during and after training. Afterward they should drink 16 to 24 ounces of fluid for every pound lost during exercise. Fluids such as water and sports drinks are preferable during matches and training sessions (suggested intakes are based on National Athletic Trainers' Association [NATA] recommendations). The amount of fluid is generally the same for each age group; however, prepubescent players should drink more water than sports drinks.

- Encourage players to replenish electrolytes, such as sodium (salt) and potassium, which are lost through sweat. The best way to replace these lost nutrients in addition to others such as carbohydrate (for energy) and protein (for muscle building) is by eating a balanced diet.

Cold

When a person is exposed to cold weather, body temperature starts to drop below normal. To counteract this reaction, the body shivers to create heat and reduces blood flow to the extremities to conserve heat in the core of the body. But no matter how effective its natural heating mechanism is, the body will better withstand cold temperatures if it is prepared to handle them. To reduce the risk of cold-related illnesses, make sure players wear appropriate protective clothing, and keep them active to maintain body heat. Also monitor the windchill factor because it can drastically affect the severity of players' responses to the weather. The windchill factor index is shown in figure 4.1.

Temperature (°F)

	0	5	10	15	20	25	30	35	40
Flesh may freeze within one minute									
40	-29	-22	-15	-8	-1	6	13	20	27
35	-27	-21	-14	-7	0	7	14	21	28
30	-26	-19	-12	-5	1	8	15	22	28
25	-24	-17	-11	-4	3	9	16	23	29
20	-22	-15	-9	-2	4	11	17	24	30
15	-19	-13	-7	0	6	13	19	25	32
10	-16	-10	-4	3	9	15	21	27	34
5	-11	-5	1	7	13	19	25	31	36

Wind speed (mph)

Windchill temperature (°F)

FIGURE 4.1   Windchill factor index.

Adapted from National Weather Service, 2009, NWS windchill chart. [Online]. Available: http://www.nws.noaa.gov/om/windchill/index.shtml [December 6, 2010].

Severe Weather

Severe weather refers to a host of potential dangers, including lightning storms, tornadoes, hail, and heavy rains. Lightning is of special concern because it can come up quickly and cause great harm or even kill. For each 5-second count from the flash of lightning to the bang of thunder, lightning is one mile away. A flash–bang of 10 seconds means lightning is two miles away; a flash–bang of 15 seconds indicates lightning is three miles away. You should stop a practice or competition for the day if lightning is three miles away or closer (15 seconds or less from flash to bang). Your school or club, league, or state association may have additional rules that you will want to consider in severe weather.

Safe places in which to take cover when lightning strikes are fully enclosed metal vehicles with the windows up, enclosed buildings, and low ground (under cover of bushes, if possible). It's not safe to be near metal objects such as flag poles, fences, light poles, goals, and metal bleachers. Also avoid trees, water, and open fields.

Cancel training when under a tornado watch or warning. If you are practicing or competing when a tornado is nearby, you should get inside a building if possible. If you cannot get into a building, lie down in a ditch or other low-lying area, or crouch near a strong building and use your arms to protect your head and neck.

The keys to handling severe weather are caution and prudence. Don't try to get that last 10 minutes of practice in if lightning is on the horizon. Don't continue to play in heavy rain. Many storms can strike both quickly and ferociously. Respect the weather and play it safe.

Air Pollution

Poor air quality and smog can present real dangers to your players. Both short- and long-term lung damage are possible from exercising in unsafe air. Although it's true that exercising in clean air is not possible in many areas, restricting activity is recommended when the air quality ratings are lower than moderate or when there is a smog alert. Your local health department or air quality control board can inform you of the air quality ratings for your area and of their recommendations for when to restrict activities.

Responding to Players' Injuries

No matter how good and thorough your prevention program is, injuries quite likely will occur. When injury does strike, chances are you will be the one in charge. The severity and nature of the injury will determine how actively involved you'll be in treating it. But regardless of how seriously a player is hurt, it is your responsibility to know what steps to take. Therefore, you must be prepared to take appropriate action and provide basic emergency care when an injury occurs.

Being Prepared

Being prepared to provide basic emergency care involves many elements, including being trained in cardiopulmonary resuscitation (CPR) and first aid and having an emergency plan.

First-Aid Kit

A well-stocked first-aid kit should include the following:

- Antibacterial soap or wipes
- Arm sling
- Athletic tape—one and a half inches
- Bandage scissors
- Bandage strips—assorted sizes
- Blood spill kit
- Cell phone
- Contact lens case
- Cotton swabs
- Elastic wraps—three inches, four inches, and six inches
- Emergency blanket
- Examination gloves (latex free)
- Eye patch
- Foam rubber—one-eighth inch, one-fourth inch, and one-half inch
- Insect sting kit
- List of emergency phone numbers
- Mirror
- Moleskin
- Nail clippers
- Oral thermometer (to determine whether a player has a fever caused by illness)
- Penlight
- Petroleum jelly
- Plastic bags for crushed ice
- Prewrap (underwrap for tape)
- Rescue breathing or CPR face mask
- Safety glasses (for assistance in first aid)
- Safety pins
- Saline solution for eyes
- Sterile gauze pads—three-inch and four-inch squares (preferably nonstick)
- Sterile gauze rolls
- Sunscreen—sun protection factor (SPF) 30 or greater
- Tape adherent and tape remover
- Tongue depressors
- Tooth saver kit
- Triangular bandages
- Tweezers

Adapted, by permission, from M. Flegel, 2008, *Sport first aid*, 4th ed. (Champaign, IL: Human Kinetics), 20.

CPR and First-Aid Training

We recommend that all coaches receive CPR and first-aid training from a nationally recognized organization such as the National Safety Council, the American Heart Association, the American Red Cross, or the American Sport Education Program (ASEP). You should be certified based on both a practical test and a written test of knowledge. Training in CPR should include obstructed airway procedures and basic life support for both children and adults.

Emergency Plan

An emergency plan is the final tool for being prepared to take appropriate action for severe or serious injuries. The plan calls for three steps:

1. **Evaluate the injured player.**

Use your CPR and first-aid training to guide you. Be sure to keep these certifications up to date. Practice your skills frequently to keep them fresh and ready to use when you need them.

2. **Call the appropriate medical personnel.**

If possible, delegate the responsibility of seeking medical help to another calm and responsible adult who attends all training sessions and matches. Write out a list of emergency phone numbers, and keep it with you at training and matches. Include the following phone numbers:

- Rescue unit
- Hospital
- Physician
- Police
- Fire department

Take each player's emergency information to every training session and match (see the sample emergency information card on page 193 of the appendix). This information includes the person to contact in case of an emergency, what types of medications the player is using, what types of drugs the player is allergic to, and so on.

Give an emergency response card (see page 194 of the appendix) to the contact person calling for emergency assistance. Having this information ready should help the contact person remain calm. You must also complete an injury report form (see page 192 of the appendix); keep one on file for any injury that occurs.

3. **Provide first aid.**

If medical personnel are not on hand at the time of the injury, provide first-aid care to the extent of your qualifications. Although your CPR and first-aid training will guide you, you must remember the following:

- Do not move the injured player if the injury is to the head, neck, or back; if a large joint (ankle, knee, elbow, shoulder) is dislocated; or if the pelvis, a rib, an arm, or a leg is fractured.

Emergency Steps

You must have a clear, well-rehearsed emergency action plan. You want to be sure you are prepared in case of an emergency because every second counts. Your emergency plan should follow this sequence:

1. Check the player's level of consciousness.
2. Send a contact person to call the appropriate medical personnel and the player's parents.
3. Send someone to wait for the rescue team and direct them to the injured player.
4. Assess the injury.
5. Administer first aid.
6. Assist emergency medical personnel in preparing the player for transportation to a medical facility.
7. Appoint someone to go with the player if the parents are not available. This person should be responsible, calm, and familiar with the player. Assistant coaches or parents are best for this job.
8. Complete an injury report form while the incident is fresh in your mind (see page 192 of the appendix).

- Calm the injured player, and keep others away from him as much as possible.
- Evaluate whether the player's breathing has stopped or is irregular; clear the airway with your fingers if necessary.
- Administer artificial respiration if the player's breathing has stopped. Administer CPR if the player's circulation has stopped.
- Remain with the player until medical personnel arrive.

Taking Appropriate Action

Proper CPR and first-aid training, a well-stocked first-aid kit, and an emergency plan prepare you to take appropriate action when an injury occurs. In the previous section, we mention the importance of providing first aid to the extent of your qualifications. Don't play doctor with injuries; sort out minor injuries that you can treat from those that need medical attention. Let's take a look at the appropriate actions for minor injuries and more serious injuries.

Minor Injuries

Although no injury seems minor to the person experiencing it, most injuries are neither life threatening nor severe enough to restrict participation. When these injuries occur, you can take an active role in their initial treatment.

Scrapes and Cuts When one of your players has an open wound, the first thing you should do is put on a pair of disposable latex-free examination gloves or some other effective blood barrier. Then follow these four steps:

1. Stop the bleeding by applying direct pressure with a clean dressing to the wound and elevating the injured area if possible. The player may be able to apply this pressure while you put on your gloves. Do not remove the dressing if it becomes soaked with blood. Instead, place an additional dressing on top of the one already in place. If bleeding continues, keep elevating the injured area above the heart and maintain pressure.

2. Cleanse the wound thoroughly once the bleeding is controlled. A good rinsing with a forceful stream of water, and perhaps light scrubbing with soap, will help prevent infection.

3. Protect the wound with sterile gauze or a bandage strip. If the player continues to participate, apply protective padding over the injured area.

4. Remove and dispose of gloves carefully to prevent yourself or anyone else from coming into contact with blood.

For bloody noses not associated with serious facial injury, have the player sit and lean slightly forward. Then pinch the player's nostrils shut. If the bleeding continues after several minutes, or if the player has a history of nosebleeds, seek medical assistance.

COACHING TIP You shouldn't let a fear of acquired immunodeficiency syndrome (AIDS) and other communicable diseases stop you from helping a player. You are only at risk if you allow contaminated blood to come in contact with an open wound on your body, so the disposable examination gloves that you wear will protect you from AIDS if one of your players carries this disease. Check with your club director, your league, or the Centers for Disease Control and Prevention (CDC) for more information about protecting yourself and your participants from AIDS.

Strains and Sprains The physical demands of soccer training and matches often result in injuries to the muscles or tendons (strains) or to the ligaments (sprains). When your players suffer minor strains or sprains, immediately apply the PRICE method of injury care:

P	Protect the player and the injured body part from further danger or trauma.
R	Rest the injured area to avoid further damage and foster healing.
I	Ice the area to reduce swelling and pain.
C	Compress the area by securing an ice bag in place with an elastic wrap.
E	Elevate the injury above heart level to keep blood from pooling in the area.

Bumps and Bruises   Soccer players inevitably make contact with each other and with the ground. If the force applied to a body part at impact is great enough, a bump or bruise will result. Many players continue playing with such sore spots, but if the bump or bruise is large and painful, you should take appropriate action. Again, use the PRICE method for injury care, and monitor the injury. If swelling, discoloration, and pain have lessened, the player may resume participation with protective padding; if not, the player should be examined by a physician.

Serious Injuries

Head, neck, and back injuries; fractures; and injuries that cause a player to lose consciousness are among a class of injuries that you cannot and should not try to treat yourself. In these cases you should follow the emergency plan outlined on page 41.

If you suspect that a player has received a blow to the head, no matter how mild the symptoms, you should view it as a serious injury. If the player has only mild symptoms, such as a headache, call the parents and have them take the player to a doctor immediately. You should alert emergency medical services (EMS) immediately if the player has lost consciousness or has impaired memory, dizziness, ringing in the ears, blood or fluid draining from the nose or ears, or blurry vision. For more information, see the "Heads Up: Concussion in Youth Sports" fact sheet, provided by the Centers for Disease Control and Prevention (www.cdc.gov), on page 45. If you suspect that a player has a spine injury, joint dislocation, or bone fracture, do not remove any of the player's equipment unless you have to do so to provide lifesaving CPR.

We do want to examine more closely, however, your role in preventing heat cramps, heat exhaustion, and heatstroke. Additionally, please refer to figure 4.2 on page 44 for an illustrative example of the signs and symptoms associated with heat exhaustion and heat stroke.

Heat Cramps   Tough training combined with heat stress and substantial fluid loss from sweating can provoke muscle cramps commonly known as heat cramps. Cramping is most common during the early part of the season, when weather is the hottest and players may be least adapted to heat. The cramp, a severe tightening of the muscle, can drop a player and prevent continued play. Dehydration, electrolyte loss, and fatigue are the contributing factors. The immediate treatment is to have the player cool off and slowly stretch the contracted muscle. The player should also consume fluids with electrolytes in order to rehydrate. The player may return to play later that same day or the next day, provided the cramp doesn't cause a muscle strain.

Heat Exhaustion   Heat exhaustion is a shocklike condition caused by dehydration and electrolyte depletion. Symptoms include headache, nausea, dizziness, chills, fatigue, and extreme thirst. Profuse sweating is a key sign of heat exhaustion. Other signs include pale, cool, clammy skin; a rapid, weak pulse; loss of coordination; and dilated pupils.

Heat exhaustion

Dizziness

Headache

Fatigue

Dehydration

Profuse sweat-
ing

Mildly
increased
body tempera-
ture

Nausea or vom-
iting

Rapid, weak
pulse

Diarrhea

Muscle cramps

Heat stroke

Dizziness

Headache

Disoriented, com-
bative, or uncon-
scious

Dehydration

Hot and wet or dry
skin

Markedly increased
body temperature

Nausea or vomit-
ing

Diarrhea

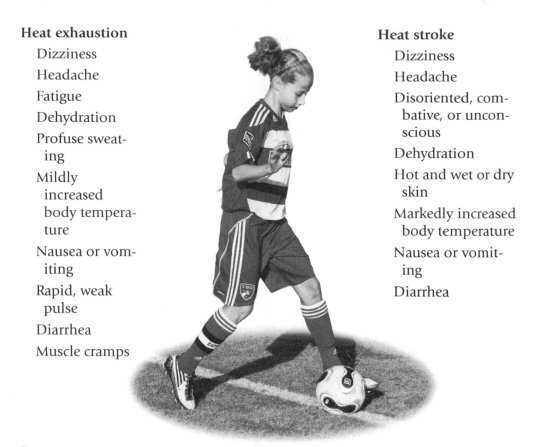

FIGURE 4.2 Signs and symptoms of heat exhaustion and heat stroke.

A player suffering from heat exhaustion should rest in a cool, shaded area; drink cool fluids, particularly those containing electrolytes; and apply ice to the neck, back, or abdomen to help cool the body. If you believe that a player has heat exhaustion, seek medical attention. Under no conditions should the player return to activity that day or before she regains all the weight lost through sweating. If the player has to see a physician, she shouldn't return to the team until she has a written release from the physician.

Heatstroke   Heatstroke is a life-threatening condition in which the body stops sweating and body temperature rises dangerously high. It occurs when dehydration causes a malfunction in the body's temperature control center in the brain. Symptoms include the feeling of being extremely hot, nausea, confusion, irritability, and fatigue. Signs include hot, dry, and flushed or red skin (this is a key sign); lack of sweat; rapid pulse; rapid breathing; constricted pupils; vomiting; diarrhea; and possibly seizures, unconsciousness, or respiratory or cardiac arrest.

If you suspect a player has heatstroke, send for emergency medical assistance immediately and cool the player as quickly as possible. Remove excess cloth-ing and equipment from the player, and lower his body temperature by using

What Is a Concussion?

A concussion is a brain injury. Concussions are caused by a bump or blow to the head. Even a "ding," "getting your bell rung," or what seems to be a mild bump or blow to the head can be serious.

You can't see a concussion. Signs and symptoms of concussion can show up right after the injury or may not appear or be noticed until days or weeks after the injury. If your child reports any symptoms of concussion, or if you notice the symptoms yourself, seek medical attention right away.

What Are the Signs and Symptoms of a Concussion?

SIGNS OBSERVED BY PARENTS OR GUARDIANS

If your child has experienced a bump or blow to the head during a game or practice, look for any of the following signs and symptoms of a concussion:

- Appears dazed or stunned
- Is confused about assignment or position
- Forgets an instruction
- Is unsure of game, score, or opponent
- Moves clumsily
- Answers questions slowly
- Loses consciousness (even briefly)
- Shows behavior or personality changes
- Can't recall events before hit or fall
- Can't recall events after hit or fall

SYMPTOMS REPORTED BY ATHLETE

- Headache or "pressure" in head
- Nausea or vomiting
- Balance problems or dizziness
- Double or blurry vision
- Sensitivity to light
- Sensitivity to noise
- Feeling sluggish, hazy, foggy, or groggy
- Concentration or memory problems
- Confusion
- Does not "feel right"

> continued

How Can You Help Children Prevent a Concussion?

Every sport is different, but there are steps children can take to protect themselves from concussion.

- Ensure that they follow their coach's rules for safety and the rules of the sport.
- Encourage them to practice good sportsmanship at all times.
- Make sure they wear the right protective equipment for their activity (such as shin guards). Protective equipment should fit properly, be well maintained, and be worn consistently and correctly.
- Learn the signs and symptoms of a concussion.

What Should You Do if You Think a Child Has a Concussion?

1. **Seek medical attention right away.** A health care professional will be able to decide how serious the concussion is and when it is safe for the child to return to sports.

2. **Keep the child out of play.** Concussions take time to heal. Don't let the child return to play until a health care professional says it's OK. Athletes who return to play too soon—while the brain is still healing—risk a greater chance of having a second concussion. Second or later concussions can be very serious. They can cause permanent brain damage, affecting the child for a lifetime.

3. **Tell other coaches about any recent concussion.** All coaches should know if a child has had a recent concussion in *any* sport. Other coaches might not know about a concussion the child suffered in another sport or activity unless you tell them.

Adapted from Centers for Disease Control and Prevention, 2007, Heads up: Concussion in youth sports: A fact sheet for parents. [Online]. Available: http://www.cdc.gov/concussion/pdf/parents_Eng.pdf [December 6, 2010].

cool, wet towels; by pouring cool water over him; or by placing him in a cold bath. Apply ice packs to the armpits, neck, back, and abdomen and between the legs. If the player is conscious, give him cool fluids to drink. If the player is unconscious, place him on his side to allow fluids and vomit to drain from the mouth. A player who has suffered heatstroke may not return to the team until he has a written release from a physician.

Protecting Yourself

When one of your players is injured, naturally your first concern is that player's well-being. Your feelings for youngsters, after all, are what made you decide to coach. Unfortunately, you must consider something else: Can you be held liable for the injury?

From a legal standpoint, a coach must fulfill nine duties. We've discussed all but planning in this chapter (planning will be discussed in chapters 5 and 11). The following is a summary of your legal duties:

1. Provide a safe environment.
2. Properly plan the activity.
3. Provide adequate and proper equipment.
4. Match players appropriately.
5. Warn of inherent risks in the sport.
6. Supervise the activity closely.
7. Evaluate players for injury or incapacitation.
8. Know emergency procedures, CPR, and first aid.
9. Keep adequate records.

In addition to fulfilling these nine legal duties, you should check your organization's insurance coverage and your own insurance coverage to make sure these policies will properly protect you from liability.

Making Training Sessions Fun and Practical

TRAINING

Every coach first needs to know the difference between practice and a training session. Practice is something players should be encouraged to do on their own time, either alone or with one or two friends. Practice involves repetition (e.g., repeatedly kicking the ball against a wall) and has obvious value. But although players do need repetition to learn a technique, when the team is together, the approach must be to have a training session. A training session is dynamic and involves correct feedback from the coach.

In the past we have placed too much emphasis on learning skills in training sessions and not enough emphasis on learning how to play skillfully—that is, learning how to use those skills in competition. The games-based approach, in contrast to the traditional drill-like approach, emphasizes first learning what to do and then learning how to do it. Moreover, the games-based approach lets kids discover what to do in the game not by your telling them but by their experiencing it. This guided discovery method of coaching empowers your players to solve the problems that arise in the game, which is a large part of the fun in learning. The games-based approach, in time, helps develop soccer-savvy players. Being soccer savvy means a player has an innate understanding of what is going on around him on a soccer field and has the talent to influence the match. Such an outcome can occur only if the player is trained in a rich soccer environment. The use of guided discovery by coaches has a positive influence on this healthy soccer experience.

Using Guided Discovery in Your Coaching

You should employ guided discovery with your players and teams on the soccer field, just as teachers do with their students in the classroom. You can do this by asking your players questions rather than overcoaching. The goal of a well-rounded player development program is to cultivate the "soccer minds" of your players. Athletes who think for themselves will develop into creative players who can anticipate and adapt within the game instead of players who are predictable and merely react to game situations. Guided discovery will force your players to think about what they are doing and why they are doing it. In general, guided discovery is not an easy thing for coaches to do. Asking players good questions at the right moments is challenging and takes years of practice to master.

Guided discovery is a process that coaches can use to introduce new skills and concepts presented in various stages of the curriculum. This process gives players an opportunity to be creative and actively participate with each new skill presented. It also gives an opportunity for the players to ask questions and practice making appropriate decisions.

The best players in the world put thought and energy into developing techniques and styles of play best suited to their individual talents. We are rarely taught conditionally. Being mindful and using imagination and creativity to learn what works best for you is what makes the difference between an average player and a champion. When players see that there's more than one technical or tactical solution to each situation, they become mindful.

To cultivate mindfulness, players and coaches must realize that information about the game looks different from different perspectives. But many coaches and players operate mindlessly, pursuing routines (drills) rather than looking for these new details.

In many ways, using guided discovery as a coaching method is more difficult than using the command style, in which the coach makes all the decisions and continually gives directed instructions to the players, who simply respond to these instructions without understanding the reasons behind them. Although the command style can be efficient, it requires no thinking on the part of the players other than memory.

To guide players, the coach must actually know the destination. To ask appropriate questions requires deeper knowledge of the training session topic by the coach. It is useful for the coach to write some questions down; these questions should appear in the written lesson plan that a coach should prepare for each training session. A characteristic of effective coaches at all levels is ongoing learning and reflection.

COACHING TIP It is often argued that effective coaching is as much an art as it is a science. The guided discovery method is a balance of the two. In a broad sense, our coaching style of the American soccer player must move away from the "sage on the stage" to the "guide on the side."

The Games-Based Approach

On the surface, it would seem to make sense to introduce soccer using the traditional approach—by first teaching the basic skills of soccer and then the tactics of the game. This approach, however, has disadvantages. First, it teaches soccer skills out of the context of the game. Kids may learn to control, shoot, pass, dribble, and head the ball. But they find it difficult to use these skills in the real match because they do not yet understand the fundamental tactics of soccer and do not appreciate how best to use their newfound skills. Second, learning skills by doing drills outside of the context of the game is downright boring. The single biggest turnoff in sports is overly organized instruction that deprives kids of their intrinsic desire to play the game. See table 5.1 on page 52 for a comparison of the use of drills versus activities in soccer.

Using activities that are gamelike at training sessions helps develop skillful, physically fit, tactically aware, and passionate players. The games-based approach helps players learn concepts of the game. Understanding game concepts (principles of play) guides players to better positioning and tactical decisions. The

TABLE 5.1   **Drills Versus Activities**

Drills	Activities
Static	Dynamic
Rigid structure	Flexible structure
Lines	Free movement
Boring	Fun
No thought	Decision making
Age inappropriate	Age appropriate

games-based approach is taught using a four-step process. These steps are as follows:

1. Play a modified game.
2. Help the players discover what they need to do to play the game successfully.
3. Teach the skills of the game.
4. Practice the skills in another game.

Step 1: Play a Modified Game

It's the first day of training; some of the kids are eager to get started, whereas others are obviously apprehensive. Some have rarely kicked a ball, most don't know the rules, and none of them know the positions in soccer. What do you do?

First, base all training sessions on the season and practice plans that you will learn more about in chapter 11. For example, if you used the traditional approach, you would have players practice kicking by lining them up for a simple kicking drill. With the games approach, however, you begin by playing an even-sided game, such as 3v3, that is modified to be developmentally appropriate for the level of the players and is designed to focus on learning a specific part of the game (such as passing).

Modifying the game emphasizes a limited number of game situations. This is one way you guide your players to discover certain tactics in the game. For instance, you have your players play a 2v2 game in a 20-by-15-yard playing area. The objective of the game is to make four passes before attempting to score. Playing the game this way forces players to think about what they have to do to keep possession of the ball.

Step 2: Help Players Understand the Game

As your players are participating in a modified game, look for the right spot to freeze the action, step in, and ask questions about errors you're seeing. When you do so, you help the players better understand the objective of the game, what they must do to reach that objective, and what specific skills they must use.

Modified Games Checklist

Modified games should be done at each training session. A modified game involves all the players in action and thinking. When developing modified games for your team, here are a few questions you should ask yourself.

- Are the games fun?
- Are the games organized?
- Are the players involved in the games?
- Are creativity and decision making being used?
- Are the spaces used appropriate?
- Is the coach's feedback appropriate?
- Are there implications for the game?

When introducing a new aspect of play for all age groups, begin teaching the topic with simple questions. The coach may need to go through a three-step questioning process:

1. Open question: This allows players to express whatever they're thinking, leaving space for them to answer thoughtfully.
2. Directed question: Part of the answer is worded within the question.
3. Closed question: The answer is within the question; a yes or no answer is a satisfactory reply.

Asking the right questions is an important part of coaching. You'll be asking your players (usually literally), "What do you need to do to succeed in this situation?" Sometimes players simply need to have more playing time to discover what they are to do, or you may need to further modify the game to make it even easier for them. This approach may take more patience on your part, but it's a powerful way for kids to learn. For example, assume your players are playing the game mentioned earlier, in which the objective is to make four passes before attempting to score, but they are having trouble. Interrupt the action and ask the following questions:

- What are you supposed to do in this game?
- What does your team have to do to keep the ball for four passes in a row?
- What do you need to do when you pass the ball to help your team keep the ball?
- Where would you move to when your teammate has the ball and you need to help him keep the ball?

COACHING TIP   Time is on your side since soccer is a long-term developmental sport. Soccer players don't fully develop until sometime in their 20s. So be patient in your coaching.

If your players have trouble understanding what to do, phrase your questions to let them choose between one option and another. For example, if you ask, "What's the fastest way to get the ball down the field?" and get answers such as "Throw it" or "Kick it," then ask, "Is it passing or dribbling?"

Asking the right questions may seem difficult at first because your players have little or no experience with the game. If you've learned sport through the traditional approach, you'll be tempted to tell your players how to play the game rather than spend time asking questions. Resist this powerful temptation to tell your players what to do. Instead, through the games-based approach and skillful questioning on your part, your players should come to realize on their own that accurate passing and receiving skills are essential to their success in controlling the ball. Rather than having told them what the critical skills are, you will have led them to this discovery—a crucial process in the games-based approach. Although it takes longer to teach a ball skill or tactic to players in the games-based approach to practice, what they learn sticks more permanently, helping develop more self-reliant and soccer-savvy players.

Step 3: Teach the Skills of the Game

Only when your players recognize the skills they need to be successful in the game do you teach specific skills through activities that focus solely on the skill at hand. This is the time when you temporarily use a more traditional approach to teaching sport skills—the IDEA approach, which we will describe in chapter 6. This coaching method is best suited to teenage players.

Step 4: Practice the Skills in Another Game

As a coach, you want your players to experience success as they're learning skills, and the best way to help them experience success early on is to create an advantage for the players. We first recommend using even-sided games (e.g., 3v3, 6v6) in step 1. The purpose behind this method is to introduce players to a situation similar to what they will experience in matches and let them discover the challenges they face in performing the necessary skill. Once the players have practiced the skill as outlined in step 3, you can then put them in another game situation—this time a game with uneven numbers (e.g., 3v1, 2v1, 3v2). The prevailing notion is that your players are more likely to experience success—for instance, in a 3v1 game, your three attacking players will be able to make four passes before attempting to score.

As players improve their skills, however, you may not need to use uneven-sided games. A 3v1 or 6v3 advantage will eventually become too easy and won't challenge your players to hone their skills. When this time comes, you can lessen the advantage. You may even decide that they're ready to train the skill in even-sided competition. The key is to set up situations in which your players experience success but are challenged at the same time. This method will take careful monitoring on your part, but having kids play uneven games as they are learning skills is a very effective way of helping them learn and improve.

The ultimate goal, of course, is to develop more soccer-savvy players who are more self-reliant during a match. Players consistently coached with the games-based approach will be more adaptable to the demands of the game, and this coaching method is also more likely to produce creative players. When the atmosphere at a training session is permeated with positive interaction, creativity, and well-timed questions, players will arrive at training already mentally alert. It is then more likely that even easily distracted players will stay on task a bit longer.

COACHING TIP   Soccer is as much an art as a science, and the game should be played attractively as well as effectively. Soccer is a game of skill, imagination, creativity, and decision making. Coaches should enhance these elements rather than stifle them.

That's the games-based approach. It immerses players in the fun of playing soccer, thus motivating them to learn the skills that will help them play the game better. Consider the difference between reciting verb conjugations in a language class but not being allowed to try to communicate in the language versus trying out some brief social communications in the language (e.g., Where's the bathroom? How do I get to the restaurant?) and thereby understanding that getting the form of the verbs right matters. Learning skills in the context of playing modified games lets players discover the whys and the hows of soccer in a fun environment. Your players will get to play more in training, and once they learn how the skills fit into their performance and enjoyment of the game, they'll be enthusiastic about working on the skills you teach them.

Gamelike Activities

The gamelike activities found here are for use in your soccer program. These activities focus on creating gamelike scenarios, distinguishing between attacking and defending teams (including goalkeeping), and setting up scoring chances. As a youth soccer coach, you will want to use gamelike activities during training sessions to keep motivation high and make the sport fun.

➤ TEAM TAG

Goal

- **U6-U12:** To develop dribbling and shielding skills
- **U14:** To warm up

Description Divide players into two or three teams of 2 to 5 players. Each player has a ball. One team tries to score by tagging members of the other two teams. Anyone tagged must bend and keep one hand on the ball. Tagging is done by touching with the hands; a player is also tagged if he loses control of his ball or crosses the boundary. Be less stringent with these rules with the U6 age group. Tagged players can be released by their teammates touching them. If one team succeeds in tagging all the other players, then another team becomes "it." The activity ends when all teams have been "it." This is a suitable activity for both the gymnasium and outdoors.

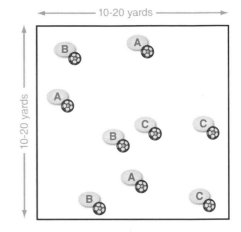

- **U6 and U8:** Play in a 10-by-10-yard playing area; 5-minute playing time.
- **U10 and U12:** Play in a 12-by-15-yard playing area; 10-minute playing time.
- **U14:** Play in a 20-by-20-yard playing area; 20-minute playing time.

Variations

- To make the activity easier for younger or less skilled players, have one team play without a ball, so no dribbling, and the players may move only by skipping or hopping.
- To make the activity more challenging for older or more skilled players, change the playing area shape to a triangle with each side 10 yards long.

➤ SLALOM RELAY

Goal   To develop dribbling skills

Description   Create small teams of equal numbers; make as many teams as needed to have all the players engaged. The playing area is a starting line with two lines of flag posts or cones about 2 yards apart as shown in the diagram. On the word "Go," the first player of each team starts dribbling. Each player must dribble the ball in between all the flag posts or cones, both out and back. The next player can go only when the first player passes him the ball over the starting line. A flying start disqualifies the team. The team to finish first is awarded 1 point. Play for 20 minutes or 10 runs per team.

- **U6:** Play in groups of 2.
- **U8:** Play in groups of 3.
- **U10-U14:** Play in groups of 4 to 6.

Variations

- Vary the dribbling technique to be used.
- To make the activity more challenging for older or more skilled players, place the flag posts at uneven distances.

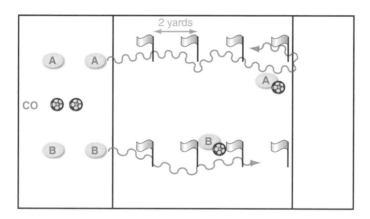

➤ SINGLE CIRCULAR TARGET

Goal   To develop the push pass. Secondary goals include improving group tactics and soccer-specific fitness.

Description   Play 3v3 in a 20-square-yard area containing a circle of 5 to 8 yards diameter, with a medicine ball or other large ball in the middle as a target, as shown in the diagram. The team in possession attacks and tries to hit the medicine ball; when possession is lost, they defend the circle. Players cannot enter the circle. If the ball goes out of play or stops within the circle, a throw-in continues the game. Hitting the medicine ball scores 1 point. After each hit, the medicine ball must be replaced on its spot. Play for a maximum of 15 minutes.

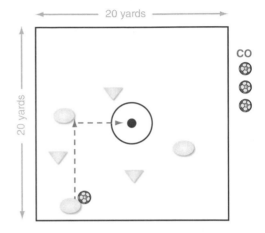

- **U6:** Let each player have a ball and play for individual points.
- **U8:** Play the activity in pairs.

Variation   The number of players may be altered: If an odd number, the extra man plays with the attackers so they have numerical superiority.

➤ SOCCER MARBLES

Goal

- **U6:** To develop dribbling skills
- **U8-U14:** To develop dribbling, shielding, and passing

Description   Play in groups of 3 on a 10-yard-square area or up to half the field to accommodate several groups. Each player has a ball. One player in each group dribbles her ball up and down the playing area. The other two try to knock the dribbler's ball away from her feet by kicking their balls against her ball. A player may kick only her ball. If a shot misses, the player must retrieve the ball herself. If she "scores" (i.e., knocks the dribbler's ball away), she changes places with the dribbler. Challenge the players to try either foot and different parts of the foot to dribble or shoot. Play for 20 minutes maximum.

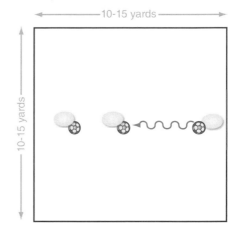

- **U6:** Each player has her own ball and tries to hit one large ball in the center of the playing area.
- **U8-U14:** Play as described.

Variation   To make the activity easier, use a smaller playing area.

➤ DRIBBLE ATTACK

Goal To develop and encourage dribbling with both feet

Description Play 3v3 in an area 30 yards long by 20 yards wide, as shown in the diagram. Attacking and defending players (3 of each) pair up and position anywhere inside the playing area (a second playing area can be set up if there are more than 6 players). Attacking players must dribble past the defending players. The defending players should try to gain possession of the ball and then (if they do) dribble past an opponent. Players may dribble in any direction inside the playing area

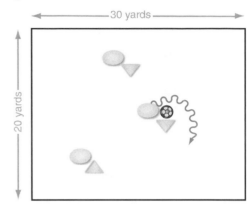

to start, and play can progress to a variation in which the coach gives the attack a direction (e.g., dribbling to a specified goal line). The attacker earns 1 point whenever she is able to dribble past a defender. The attacker is allowed to pass past a defender in an effort to advance the ball but receives no points for doing so.

- **U6:** Play two 2-minute rounds; focus only on attackers properly dribbling past defenders.
- **U8:** Play two 2-minute rounds.
- **U10:** Play three 3-minute rounds.
- **U12:** Play four 4-minute rounds.
- **U14:** Play five 5-minute rounds.

Variations

- To make the activity easier for younger or less skilled players, play 3v2 or 2v1.
- To make the activity more challenging for older or more skilled players, award an additional point for attacking players who dribble past a defender while using their weak foot, or award points only for dribbling past a defender with the weak foot.

➤ SOCCER SKITTLES

Goal   To practice passing with the inside of the foot. Secondary goals include improving receiving and group defending skills; developing principles of attack and soccer-specific fitness; and practicing dynamic game situations.

Description   Play 3v3 or 4v4 in a playing area 40 yards long by 20 yards wide, with an area 3 yards wide along each side. Place three "skittles" (cones, bowling pins) at an equal distance inside both of these areas as shown in the diagram. Adapt the size of the playing area and the duration of play to the age group. A team defends its own skittles and attempts to knock over its opponent's skittles. If a team loses the ball, puts the ball out of play, or scores, the other team gains possession. Players cannot enter the skittle area. Skittles that are knocked over remain down to show the score. Play for 20 minutes maximum.

- **U6:** Begin by asking each player to play on his own, one ball per player. In the final round, play 3v3 with one ball.
- **U8:** Begin the activity with the players divided into pairs, one ball per pair. In the final round, play 4v4 with one ball.
- **U10-U14:** Play the activity as described.

Variation   To make the activity more difficult, restrict which foot can be used for the shot at the skittle.

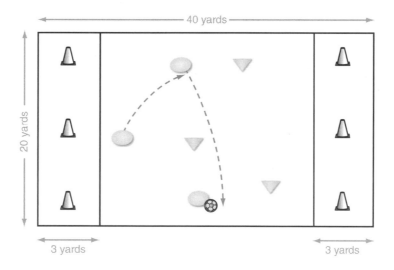

➤ THE LONG BOMB

Goal To develop and encourage long passing techniques by getting the ball to the target player

Description Play 4v4 in a playing area with two zones, one at each end. The activity begins in the center of the area, and players must pass from behind the zone line. Teams are awarded 1 point for a successful pass into a zone. After a successful pass, the activity restarts with a free pass from within the zone to a player from the scoring team, and defenders must freeze while the free pass is made. If the ball goes out of play, possession changes and the activity restarts with a free pass. Again, defenders must freeze while the free pass is made. Players may not make a pass to a zone directly from a restart.

- **U6:** Use a 20-by-20-yard playing area with a 5-yard zone at each end. Play for 5 minutes or until 3 points are scored.
- **U8:** Use a 30-by-20-yard playing area with a 5-yard zone at each end. Play for 10 minutes or until 5 points are scored.
- **U10-U14:** Use a 40-by-20-yard playing area with a 10-yard zone at each end. Two additional players position within the two zones and act as neutral target players who receive passes from other players. Play for 15 minutes or until 10 points are scored.

Variations

- To make the activity easier for younger or less skilled players, allow players to score points by lofting or driving the ball into the zone.
- To make the activity more challenging for older or more skilled players, give each player only two touches to play when in possession, or increase the field size to 60 by 30 yards, or play 5v5.

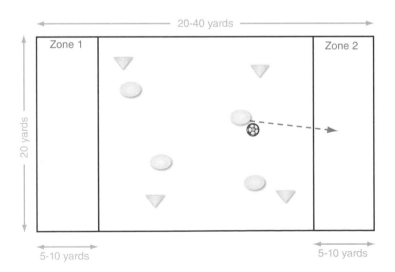

➤ HEADS UP

Goal   To develop heading skills

Description   Play 3v3 in a 20-square-yard area, with one goal set up in the center of one touchline, as shown in the diagram. Attacking and defending teams each consist of 3 players; the defending team utilizes a goalkeeper as one of its 3 players. The attacking team has the ball, and the activity begins in the center of the playing area. When play begins, the attacking team attempts to score as many goals as possible in 6 minutes. A kicked goal is worth 1 point. A goal scored by heading is worth 2 points. After a goal, the defending team restarts play with a goal kick.

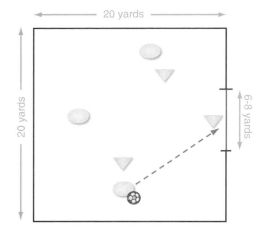

Teams play the game normally during minutes 1, 3, and 5. During minutes 2, 4, and 6, the coach calls, "Heads up!" to indicate a minute of heading for the team on attack. One specific player is designated the header; he will receive tosses from a teammate and attempt to head the ball into the goal past the goalkeeper as many times as possible during the allotted minute. All other players will freeze during this time. Switch teams after 6 minutes of play or when 10 points have been made.

- **U6-U10:** This activity is not appropriate for these age groups.
- **U12:** Use a 6-yard-wide goal.
- **U14:** Use an 8-yard-wide goal.

Variations

- To make the activity easier for younger or less skilled players, eliminate the goalkeeper during the heading sessions.
- To make the activity more challenging for older or more skilled players, play with an even number of field players.

➤ HOT POTATO

Goal   To develop receiving with the foot, thigh, or chest

Description   Players position in a playing area as shown in the diagram. Play begins with a drop ball. The focus is on controlling the ball; there are no goals at which to shoot. Award 1 point for every pass received and controlled by the foot and 2 points for every pass received and controlled by the thigh or chest. Any ball that goes out of bounds is put back into play with a throw-in.

- **U6:** Play 1v1 up to 3v3 in a 15-by-10-yard playing area. Focus on ground balls, and use only kick-ins.
- **U8:** Play 2v2 up to 3v3 in a 20-by-15-yard playing area. Focus primarily on ground balls, with occasional balls in the air. Receiving the ball on the bounce is quite acceptable at this age. Use a mix of mostly kick-ins and a few throw-ins.
- **U10-U14:** Play 3v3 in a 35-by-25-yard playing area. Focus on both ground balls and balls in the air.

Variations

- To make the activity easier for younger or less skilled players, play 3v1 or 4v2, or increase the playing area to 40 by 30 yards.
- To make the activity more challenging for older or more skilled players, play 2v3 or 3v4, or decrease the playing area to 30 by 20 yards.

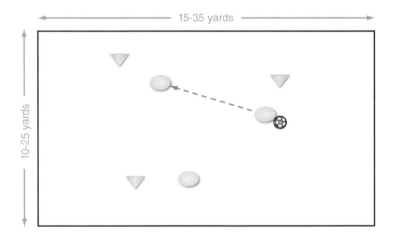

➤ CORNER KICKING

Goal   To attack and defend at corner kicks

Description   Play 4v4 in a playing area 20 yards long by 40 yards wide, with a goal set up along the length of the area on one side as shown in the diagram. The attacking team gets four corner kicks (one for each player), attempting to score on each kick. Award 2 points for a goal scored directly off a corner kick and 1 point for a goal scored before the defense can control the ball. To focus on defense, you may give points only to the defense—award 1 point for not allowing a score on a corner kick. After each player has made a kick, switch teams and repeat the sequence of kicks.

- **U6:** This activity is not appropriate for this age group.
- **U8:** Use a 6-yard-wide goal and no goalkeepers.
- **U10-U14:** Use an 8-yard-wide goal, and utilize a goalkeeper as one of the attacking players.

Variations

- To make the activity easier for younger or less skilled players, play 5v3 or 4v2, or don't allow the defense to touch the ball first, even if they are able to do so.
- To make the activity more challenging for older or more skilled players, play 4v5 or 3v5, or award points only for direct scoring from corner kicks.

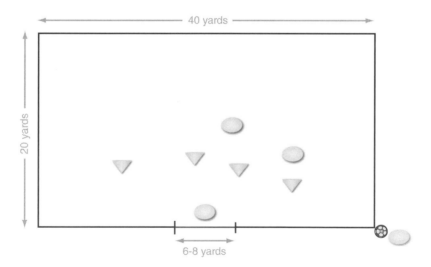

➤ THROW-IN

Goal   To develop throw-in skills. Secondary goals include developing mobility, using the width and depth of the field, and improving teamwork.

Description   Play 5v5 on a playing field no larger than 40 yards long by 20 yards wide. Teams try to attack the opposition goal and win points by skillful position-ing. The players pass the ball and score goals with legal throw-ins (both hands behind the head and both feet firmly on the ground). Players cannot move when they have the ball. The opposition gets the ball if an interception is made, if the ball goes out of play, or if the ball is played with the feet. Corners are thrown in. There are no proper goalkeepers and no offside. Play for 30 minutes maximum.

- **U6 and U8:** This activity is not appropriate for these age groups.
- **U10-U14:** Play as described.

Variations
- To make the activity more difficult, throw-ins at goal can only be made out-side the goal area.
- Use normal age-appropriate goals with goalkeepers.

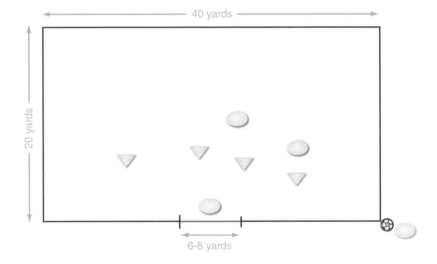

➤ OBLIGATORY SHOOTING

Goal   To improve instep shooting. Secondary goals include learning the role of first and second attacker; training for passing, receiving, blocking shots, tackling, and intercepting passes; and improving group defending, communication, tactical awareness, mental focus, and match fitness.

Description   Play in teams of 2 to 5, with one neutral keeper, in a playing area as small as double the age-appropriate penalty area and as large as half the field. Use one age-appropriate goal. One team attacks and tries to score goals as the defense tries to avoid conceding goals. The keeper starts the activity with an impartial throw or goal kick. The first player controls the ball and passes to a teammate, who is then obliged to shoot. Ball possession changes after interceptions, balls out of play, or errors in play (e.g., someone other than the second player shoots the ball) as well as after any foul. If the keeper gathers the ball or if it goes over the goal line, he restarts the game with a goal kick, as he does if a goal is scored. Play for 30 minutes maximum.

- **U6 and U8:** This activity is not appropriate for these age groups.
- **U10-U14:** Play as described with the age-appropriate field dimensions and goal.

Variation   Establish which foot and which type of kick should be used for shooting. This makes the activity more challenging. Please note that if there are only 2 players on each team, the first player must shoot. If more than 5, the third player must shoot.

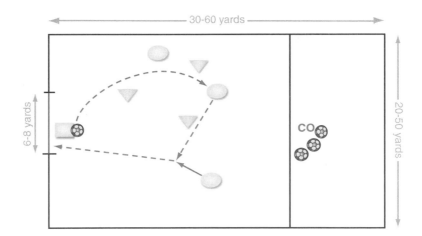

➤ **CAPTAINS**

Goal   To improve running off the ball. Secondary goals include improving passing, receiving, shielding, dribbling, and covering skills.

Description   Play in teams of 4 to 6 on one-third of an age-appropriate field. Teams elect a captain. The captains of each team should be clearly recognizable (e.g., cap or different color training bib). One team starts trying to pass the ball to its captain. The other team puts its effort into preventing this and to winning the ball. When a team manages to pass the ball to its captain, it is awarded 1 point. The opposition is given the ball if a player manages to intercept, or if the ball goes out of play, or if a point is scored. Captains are switched after a certain time, depending on their stamina, since they have to run the most. Play for 20 minutes maximum.

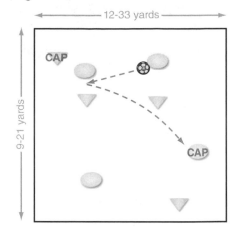

- **U6:** This activity is not appropriate for this age group.
- **U8:** The coach may need to play with one team to help the children see the concept. After a set period of time, the coach should play with the other team.
- **U10-U14:** Play as described in an age-appropriate training area.

Variation   The team that wins 1 point retains the ball and continues the activity. This makes the activity more challenging.

➤ MONKEY ON THEIR BACKS

Goal   To develop marking skills

Description   Play 2v2 or 3v3 in a playing area as shown in the diagram. Each team has an end line to defend; the two end lines act as goals for the purpose of this game. Play begins in the middle of the playing area with a drop ball. Players must stay between the attacker with the ball and the defender's goal. Only the defense can earn points. Award 1 point when an attacker cannot advance the ball past her defender, either by passing or dribbling (award the point when the attacker is forced to pass back to a teammate) and 2 points if a defender intercepts or otherwise takes away the ball. When the ball goes out of bounds, play is restarted with either a kick-in or throw-in. Play to 5 points and then switch ends.

- **U6 and U8:** Use a 20-by-10-yard playing area. Play is restarted with a kick-in.
- **U10-U14:** Use a 30-by-15-yard playing area. Play is restarted with a throw-in.

Variations

- To make the activity easier for younger or less skilled players, allow the attacking team more time by permitting the defense to pressure only in their half of the field. Or shorten the number of yards needed to score points by decreasing the size of the playing area.
- To make the activity more challenging for more skilled players, allow the attacking team less time by permitting the defending team to pressure full field. Or lengthen the number of yards needed to score points by increasing the size of the playing area.

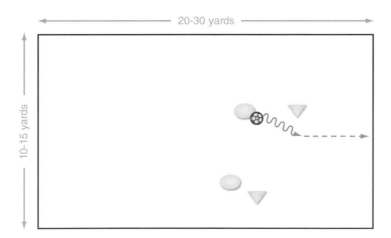

➤ THE DUEL

Goal   To develop tackling techniques

Description   Players posi- tion in a playing area with two 5-yard-wide goals and a 4-yard-long shooting zone set up at each end, as shown in the diagram. Play begins at midfield, and the 2 defend- ers try to tackle the ball while the 2 attacking players try to move the ball down the field. Once inside the 4-yard shooting zone, the attacking players can shoot on goal. If a goal is scored the ball goes to the opposing team, and

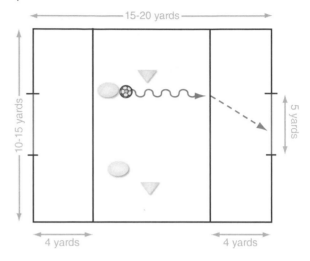

play restarts with a kick-in or throw-in at its own end line. Award 2 points for any ball that is tackled and 1 point if the ball leaves the field and is awarded to the defending team.

- **U6 and U8:** Play 1v1 in a 15-by-10-yard playing area. Play is restarted with a kick-in.

- **U10-U14:** Play 2v2 in a 20-by-15-yard playing area. Play is restarted with a throw-in.

Variations

- To make the activity easier for younger or less skilled players, reduce the length of the field or play 2v3.

- To make the activity more challenging for older or more skilled players, create a dividing line halfway down the field, and require the defender to tackle in the opponent's half of the field only. Or create a dividing line halfway down the field, allow the attacker to pass back to a teammate to relieve pressure from the defender, and require the defender to stay at the halfway line until the attacker gets the ball back from the teammate.

➤ CRUNCH TIME

Goal To develop block-tackling and poke-tackling techniques

Description Players position in a playing area with a goal set up at each end, as shown in the diagram. The attacking team starts play with a kickoff. Award 1 point for each block or poke tackle made by the defense. After the defense makes a tackle, the ball is returned to the attackers.

- **U6:** Play 1v1 in a 15-by-10-yard playing area with a 6-yard-wide goal; 5-minute playing time.
- **U8-U14:** Play 2v4 or 3v5 (or other lopsided configuration with more players on the defending side) in a 30-by-15-yard playing area with a 6-yard-wide goal or 8-yard-wide goal for U14; 10-minute playing time.

Variations

- To make the activity easier for younger or less skilled players, decrease the size of the field or add a defender.
- To make the activity more challenging for older or more skilled players, increase the size of the field or add another offensive player.

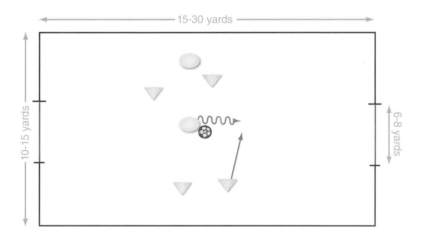

➤ TRIANGULAR GOAL GAME

Goal   To practice intercepting passes. Secondary goals include covering the goal, tackling, developing defensive posture, and improving recovery and tracking runs.

Description   Play 3v3 in a playing area from 20 square yards to 40 square yards, depending on the age group. The playing area is divided into two halves, each containing three goalmouths (three flag posts placed in a triangle), as shown in the diagram. One team attacks its opponent's half with the objective of scoring through any side of the triangular goal, while one player of the other team each defends one side of the goal. A goal is scored whenever the ball crosses any of the three goal lines. A shot may be taken only from inside the attacking half. Each player is responsible for one goal line. His teammates may not come to his aid by leaving their own goal untended. Ball possession changes after interceptions or saves, balls out of play, fouls, and goals. The width of the goals and the length of the periods played should suit the stamina and ability of the players. Play 10 to 30 minutes depending on the age group.

- **U6:** This activity is not appropriate for this age group.
- **U8:** The coach may need to play with one team to help the children see the concept. After a set period of time, the coach should play with the other team.
- **U10-U14:** Play as described for a duration appropriate for the age group.

Variations

- To make the activity easier for younger or less skilled players, all players can defend all goal lines.
- To make the activity more challenging for older or more skilled players, do not allow handballs.

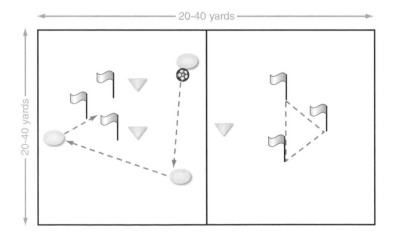

➤ NARROW ENOUGH

Goal To develop the goalkeeper's ability to narrow the shooting angle

Description Play 3v1 in a 30-square-yard area with a goal set up at one end, as shown in the diagram. The attacking team consists of 3 players, and the defending team consists of 1 goalkeeper. The 3 attacking players pass among each other, attempting to score. The objective is to try to shoot from the side, forcing the goalkeeper to narrow the angle to stop the shot. Award the attack 1 point for a goal scored head-on and 2 points for a goal scored from either side. Award the goalkeeper 1 point for every shot stopped. After shots are completed, rotate keepers.

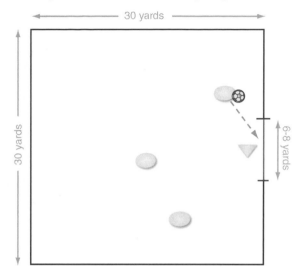

- **U6 and U8:** This activity is not appropriate for these age groups.
- **U10:** Use a 6-yard-wide goal; 5 shots on goal or a 5- to 10-minute playing time.
- **U12 and U14:** Use an 8-yard-wide goal; 7 shots on goal or a 10- to 15-minute playing time.

Variations
- To make the activity easier for younger or less skilled players, call out the side for the shot to come from, increase the shooting distance, or use a smaller goal.
- To make the activity more challenging for older or more skilled players, reduce the shooting distance, use a bigger goal, or add a player who tries to score goals from rebounds if the goalkeeper fails to deal with the shot effectively.

➤ OVER THE TOP

Goal   To develop the ability to distribute the ball by punting it

Description   Play 3v3 in a playing area divided into zones, with a goal set up at one end as shown in the diagram. The attacking team consists of 3 players, and the defending team consists of 3 players, the latter utilizing a goalkeeper as one of its players. The attacking team attacks the goal, and the defending team defends it. The defense is awarded points for shots that the keeper stops and successfully distributes by punting the ball: 1 point if the ball lands within zone 2 (the middle 20 yards), 2 points if the ball lands within zone 3 (the farthest 20 yards), and 1 additional point for any punt that is controlled by one of the keeper's teammates. After each defender has had three chances to punt, switch teams.

- **U6 and U8:** This activity is not appropriate for these age groups.
- **U10:** Play in a 40-by-20-yard playing area with 10-yard zones; use a 6-yard-wide goal.
- **U12 and U14:** Play in a 60-by-20-yard playing area with 20-yard zones; use an 8-yard-wide goal.

Variations

- To make the activity easier for younger or less skilled players, instruct the attackers to kick the ball easily to the keeper to begin play and not to try to score a goal, or reduce the length of the field.
- To make the activity more challenging for older or more skilled players, give keepers a point for catching the ball cleanly, or increase the length of the field.

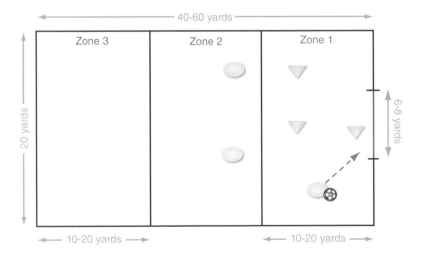

Teaching and
Shaping Skills

SKILLS

Coaching

soccer is about teaching kids how to play the game by teaching them skills, strategies, fitness, fair play, and values. It's also about coaching players before, during, and after matches. Teaching and coaching are closely related, but there are important differences. In this chapter we focus on principles of teaching, especially teaching technical and tactical skills. But these principles apply to teaching fitness concepts and values as well. Armed with these principles, you will be able to design effective and efficient practices and will understand how to deal with misbehavior. Then you will be able to teach the skills and tactics necessary to be successful in soccer, which are outlined in chapters 7, 8, and 9.

Teaching Soccer Skills

Technique is the body's mechanical execution in order to manipulate the ball (e.g., receiving, catching, shooting, dribbling, or deflecting). It is one of the four components of the game and leads to ball skill. Skill is being able to execute a technique under the pressure of opponents in tight spaces and most likely on the move. Without ball skill, a player cannot execute tactics.

Many people believe that the only qualification needed to teach a skill is to have performed it. Although it's helpful to have performed the skill, teaching it successfully requires much more than that. Even if you haven't performed the skill before, you can still learn to teach successfully with the useful acronym IDEA:

I	Introduce the skill.
D	Demonstrate the skill.
E	Explain the skill.
A	Attend to players practicing the skill.

Introduce the Skill

Players, especially those who are young and inexperienced, need to know what skill they are learning and why they are learning it. You should therefore use the following three steps every time you introduce a skill to your players:

1. Get your players' attention.
2. Name the skill.
3. Explain the importance of the skill.

Get Your Players' Attention

Because youngsters are easily distracted, you must make them sit up and take notice. Some coaches use interesting news items or stories, others use jokes, and still others simply project enthusiasm to get their players to listen. Whatever method you use, speak slightly above your normal volume, and look your players in the eye when you speak.

Also, position players so that they can see and hear you. Arrange them in a group, facing you (make sure they aren't looking into the sun or at a distracting activity). Be sure they are all in your field of vision before you begin to speak.

> **COACHING TIP**   Writing out in detail each skill you will teach clarifies what you will say and how you will demonstrate each skill to your players. The Skills School Manual, with key points on all soccer skills, is available at www.usyouthsoccer.org.

Name the Skill

Use the names of the ball skills as you find them in US Youth Soccer's Skills School Manual. Doing so prevents confusion and enhances communication among your players. When you introduce the new skill, call it by name several times so that the players automatically correlate the name with the skill in later discussions.

Explain the Importance of the Skill

As Rainer Martens, the founder of ASEP, has said, "The most difficult aspect of coaching is this: Coaches must learn to let athletes learn. Sport skills should be taught so they have meaning to the child, not just meaning to the coach." Although the importance of a skill may be apparent to you, your players may be less able to see how the skill will help them become better soccer players. Offer them a reason for learning the skill, and describe how it relates to more advanced skills. This step will increase in importance for the U10 age group and up. For the U6 and U8 age groups, you may want to use imagination and storytelling to introduce skills into gamelike activities.

Demonstrate the Skill

The demonstration step is the most important part of teaching sport skills to players who may never have done anything closely resembling it. They need to see how the skill is performed, not just to hear a description. If you are unable to perform the skill correctly, ask an assistant coach, one of your players, an older player in your club, or someone more skilled to demonstrate it.

These tips will make your demonstrations more effective:

- Use correct form.
- Demonstrate the skill several times.
- Slow the action, if possible, during one or two performances so that players can see every movement involved in the skill.
- Perform the skill at different angles so that your players can get a range of perspectives.
- Demonstrate the skill with both sides of the body, as applicable.
- Do not speak during the demonstration; save your words for before and after you demonstrate.

Explain the Skill

Players learn more effectively when they're given a brief explanation of the skill along with the demonstration. Use simple terms and, if possible, relate the skill to those previously learned. Ask your players whether they understand your description. A good technique is to ask the team to repeat your explanation. Ask questions such as "What are you going to do first?" and "Then what?" Should players look confused or uncertain, repeat your explanation and demonstration. If possible, use different words so that your players can try to understand the skill from a different perspective. Remember, too, that whenever you bring players into a group to make a coaching point, you must be clear, correct, and concise.

Complex skills often are better understood when you explain them in more manageable parts. For instance, if you want to teach your players how to change direction when they dribble the ball, you might take the following steps:

1. Show players a correct performance of the entire skill, and explain its function in soccer. Now have your players participate in a brief activity that accentuates the skill.

2. Break down the skill, and point out its component parts to your players.

3. Have players perform each of the component skills you have already taught them, such as dribbling while running, changing speed, and changing direction. Now play the same activity as you did in step 1.

4. After players have demonstrated their ability to perform the separate parts of the skill in sequence, explain the entire skill again.

5. Have players practice the skill in gamelike conditions.

Young players have short attention spans, and a long demonstration or explanation of a skill may cause them to lose focus. Therefore, spend no more than a few minutes altogether on the introduction, demonstration, and explanation phases. Then involve the players in activities that call on them to perform the skill.

> **COACHING TIP**   Demonstrations should take 1 minute or less in order to keep the attention of the players. For the U8 and U10 age groups, try to keep demonstrations at 30 seconds or less, and for the U6 age group, try to keep demonstrations at 15 seconds or less.

Attend to Players Practicing the Skill

If the skill you selected was within your players' capabilities and you have done an effective job of introducing, demonstrating, and explaining it, your players should be ready to attempt the skill. Some players may need to be physically guided through the movements during their first few attempts. Walking unsure athletes through the skill in this way will help them gain confidence to perform it on their own. Please be aware that trial and error is an important part of learning any physical skill. Be patient as players make mistakes learning a skill; many soccer skills can take years to fully master.

How to Properly Run Your Activities

Before running an activity that teaches technique, you should do the following:

- Name the activity.
- Explain the skill you are teaching.
- Organize the equipment and the players correctly.
- Explain what the activity will accomplish. This step is important for the U12 and older age groups.
- State the command that will start the activity.
- State the command that will end the activity.

Once you have introduced and repeated the activity a few times in this manner, you will find that merely calling out its name is sufficient. Your players will automatically line up in the proper position to run the activity and practice the skill.

Look at the entire skill, and then break it down into fundamental components. For example, when teaching the push pass, your activity sequence could consist of the following steps:

1. Stance
2. Eye on the ball
3. Back swing of the kicking leg
4. Forward swing of the kicking leg
5. Proper contact with the ball
6. Follow-through of the kicking leg
7. Pattern recognition and pattern reaction

Your teaching duties, though, don't end when all your players have demonstrated that they understand how to perform a skill. As you help your players improve their skills, your teaching role is in fact just beginning. A significant part of coaching consists of closely observing the hit-and-miss trial performances of your players. You will sharpen players' skills by detecting errors and correcting them with positive feedback. Keep in mind that your positive feedback will have a great influence on your players' motivation to practice and improve their performances. Focus your attention and comments on catching the kids doing well rather than on the inevitable miscues.

Remember, too, that some players may need individual instruction. So set aside a time before, during, or after training to give individual help.

Helping Players Improve Skills

After you have successfully taught your players the fundamentals of a skill, your focus will be on helping them improve it. Players learn skills and improve them at different rates, so don't get frustrated if progress seems slow. Instead, help them progress by shaping their skills and detecting and correcting errors.

Shaping Players' Skills

One of your principal teaching duties is to reward positive effort and behavior—in terms of successful skill execution—when you see it. A player makes a good pass in training, and you immediately say, "That's the way to drive through it! Good follow-through!" Such comments, plus a smile and a thumbs-up gesture, go a long way toward reinforcing skill technique in that player. However, sometimes you may have a long dry spell before you see correct techniques to reinforce. It's difficult to reward players when they don't execute skills correctly. How can you shape their skills if this is the case?

Molding skills takes practice on your players' part and patience on yours. Expect them to make errors. Telling the player who made the great pass that he did a good job doesn't ensure that he'll have the same success next time. Seeing inconsistency in your players' technique can be frustrating. It's even more challenging to stay positive when your players repeatedly perform a skill incorrectly or have a lack of enthusiasm for learning. It can be quite frustrating to see players who seemingly don't heed your advice and continue to make the same mistakes.

Please know that it is normal to get frustrated sometimes when teaching skills. Nevertheless, part of successful coaching is controlling this frustration. Instead of getting upset, use these six guidelines for shaping skills:

1. Think small initially.

Reward the first signs of behavior that approximate what you want. Then reward closer and closer approximations of the desired behavior. In short, use your reward power to shape the behavior you seek.

2. Break skills into small steps.

For instance, in learning to dribble, one of your players does well in watching for defenders around the ball, but she's careless with dribbling the ball and doesn't effectively shield it from defenders. She often has the ball too far away from her as she dribbles, or she runs too fast and loses control of it. Reinforce the correct technique of watching for defenders, and teach her how to keep the ball close. Once she masters these skills, focus on getting her to run at a speed at which she can control the ball.

3. Develop one component of a skill at a time.

Don't try to shape two components of a skill at once. For example, in receiving a ball with the inside of the foot, players must first stop the ball and then redirect or turn it by trapping and controlling it with the foot. Players should focus initially on one aspect (stopping the ball with the arch of the inside of the foot while cushioning it by pulling the receiving leg back slightly) and then on the other (turning the ball by controlling it with the foot). When players have problems mastering a skill, it's often because they're trying to improve two or more components at once. Help these players isolate a single component. As each component of a technique improves, then combine those components into a sequence of movements that becomes a skill.

4. Use reinforcement only occasionally, for the best examples.

By focusing only on the best examples, you will help players continue to improve once they've mastered the basics. Using occasional reinforcement during training allows players to have more contact time with the ball rather than to constantly stop and listen to the coach. Soccer skills are best learned through a lot of random repetition, such as gamelike activities, and the coach needs to make the best use of team training time by allowing the players as much time with the ball as possible.

5. Relax your reward standards.

As players focus on mastering a new skill or attempt to integrate it with other skills, their old, well-learned skills may temporarily degenerate, and you may need to relax your expectations. For example, a player who has learned how to receive a pass along the ground with the inside of the foot is now learning how to combine that skill with turning at the same time as he receives. While learning to combine the two skills and getting the timing down, he may have poor control of the ball. A similar degeneration of ball skills may occur during growth spurts, typically between ages 11 and 14, while the coordination of muscles, tendons, and ligaments catches up to the growth of bones.

6. Go back to the basics.

If, however, a well-learned skill degenerates for long, you may need to restore it by going back to the basics. If necessary, practice the skill using an activity in which the players have a larger training area and less pressure from opponents so that they can refresh the skill.

COACHING TIP Beginning with the U10 age group, coaches can ask players to self-coach. With the proper guidance and a positive team environment, young players can think about how they perform a skill and how they might be able to perform it better. Self-coaching is best done at practice, where a player can experiment with learning new skills.

Detecting and Correcting Errors

Good coaches recognize that players make two types of errors: learning errors and performance errors. Learning errors are ones that occur because players don't know how to perform a skill; that is, they have not yet developed the correct motor pattern in the brain to perform a particular skill. Players make performance errors not because they don't know how to execute the skill but because they have made a mistake in executing what they do know. There is no easy way to know whether a player is making learning or performance errors, and part of the art of coaching is being able to sort out which type of error each mistake is. As Yankee legend Yogi Berra once said, "You can observe a lot by watching."

The process of helping players correct errors begins with your observing and evaluating their performances to determine whether the mistakes are learning or performance errors. Carefully watch your players to see whether they routinely make the errors in both training and match settings, or whether the errors tend to occur only in match settings. If the latter is the case, then your players are making performance errors. For performance errors, you need to look for the reasons your players are not performing as well as they should; perhaps they are nervous, or maybe they get distracted by the match setting. If the mistakes are learning errors, then you need to help them learn the skill, which is the focus of this section.

When correcting learning errors, there is no substitute for the coach knowing skills well. The better you understand a skill—not only how one performs it correctly but also what causes learning errors—the more helpful you will be in correcting mistakes.

One of the most common coaching mistakes is to provide inaccurate feedback and advice on how to correct errors. Don't rush into error correction; wrong feedback or poor advice will hurt the learning process more than no feedback or advice at all. If you are uncertain about the cause of the problem or how to correct it, continue to observe and analyze until you are more sure. As a rule, you should see the error repeated several times before attempting to correct it.

Correct One Error at a Time

Suppose Jill, one of your forwards, is having trouble with her shooting. She's doing most things well, but you notice that she's not keeping her toes pointed down as she strikes the ball, and she often approaches the ball sort of sideways, with her hips not square to the target. What do you do?

First, decide which error to begin with; players learn more effectively when they attempt to correct one error at a time. Determine whether one error is causing the other; if so, have the player correct that error first because it may eliminate the other error. In Jill's case, however, neither error is causing the other. In such cases, players should correct the error that is easiest to correct and that will bring the greatest improvement when remedied. For Jill, it probably means kicking with the toes of the kicking foot pointed down. Improving the kick will likely motivate her to correct the other error.

Use Positive Feedback to Correct Errors

The positive approach to correcting errors includes emphasizing what to do instead of what not to do. Use compliments, praise, rewards, and encouragement to correct errors. Acknowledge correct performance as well as efforts to improve. By using positive feedback, you can help your players feel good about themselves and promote a strong desire to achieve. Give them praise when it has been earned. The younger they are, the more praise they need.

When you're working with one player at a time, the positive approach to correcting errors includes four steps:

1. Praise effort and proper performance.

Praise the player for trying to perform a skill correctly and for performing any parts of it correctly. Do so immediately after he performs the skill, if possible. Keep the praise simple: "Good try," "Way to stay focused," "Good extension," or "That's the way to follow through." You can also use nonverbal feedback such as smiling, clapping your hands, or any facial or body expression that shows approval.

Make sure you're sincere with your praise. Don't indicate that a player's effort was good when it wasn't. Usually a player knows whether he has made a sincere effort to perform the skill correctly and perceives undeserved praise for what it is—untruthful feedback to make him feel good. Likewise, don't indicate that a player's performance was correct when it wasn't.

2. Give simple and precise feedback to correct errors.

Don't burden a player with a long or detailed explanation of how to correct an error. Give just enough feedback that the player can correct one error at a time. Before giving feedback, recognize that some players readily accept it immediately after the error, whereas others respond better if you delay the correction slightly. Be brief while making your coaching point, and get the player back into action quickly.

For errors that are complicated to explain and difficult to correct, try the following:

- Explain and demonstrate what the player should have done. Do not demonstrate what the player did wrong.
- Explain the causes of the error if they aren't obvious.
- Explain why you are recommending the correction you have selected if it's not obvious.

3. Make sure the player understands your feedback.

If the player doesn't understand your feedback, she won't be able to correct the error. First ask her to show you how to do the skill again. Then if needed ask her to repeat the feedback and to explain and demonstrate how she will use it. If the player can't do this, be patient and present your feedback again. Then have her repeat the feedback after you're finished.

4. Provide an environment that motivates the player to improve.

Your players won't always be able to correct their errors immediately, even if they do understand your feedback. Encourage them to hang tough and stick with it when adjustments are difficult or when they seem discouraged. For more difficult corrections, remind them that it will take time and that the improvement will happen only if they work at it. Encourage players who have little self-confidence. Say something like this: "You were dribbling smoother today; with practice, you'll be able to keep the ball closer to you and shield it from defenders." Such support can motivate a player to continue to refine his dribbling skills.

Other players may be very self-motivated and need little help from you in this area; with them you can practically ignore step 4 when correcting an error. Although motivation comes from within, try to provide an environment of positive instruction and encouragement to help your players improve.

COACHING TIP Players are also more motivated to learn when exposed to a higher level of play. The youth soccer environment has devolved into a situation that limits interaction between age groups (and, on occasion, genders). By allowing this to happen, we miss out on opportunities for players to help one another grow into the game and learn from each other. Coaches should organize training sessions in which more experienced players are available to give younger players encouragement and pointers.

A final note on correcting errors: Team sports such as soccer provide unique challenges in this endeavor. How do you provide individual feedback in a group setting using a positive approach? Instead of yelling across the field to correct an error (and embarrassing the player), pull that player aside. Then make the correction beside the training area. This type of feedback has several advantages:

- The player will be more receptive to one-on-one feedback.
- The other players are active and still practicing skills, unable to hear your discussion.
- Because the rest of the team is still playing, you'll feel compelled to make your comments simple and concise, which is more helpful to the player.

This procedure doesn't mean you can't also use the team setting to give specific, positive feedback. You can do so to emphasize proper group and individual performances. Use this team feedback approach only for positive statements, though. Save corrections for individual discussion.

Dealing With Misbehavior

Children misbehave at times; it's only natural. Following are two ways you can respond to misbehavior, through extinction or discipline.

Extinction

Ignoring misbehavior—neither rewarding it nor disciplining it—is called extinction. This approach can be effective under certain circumstances. In some situations, disciplining young people's misbehavior only encourages them to act up further because of the recognition they get. Ignoring misbehavior teaches youngsters that it is not worth your attention.

Sometimes, though, you cannot wait for a behavior to fizzle out. When players cause danger to themselves or others or disrupt the activities of others, you need to take immediate action. Tell the offending player that the behavior must stop and that discipline will follow if it doesn't. If the child doesn't stop misbehaving after the warning, follow through with discipline.

Extinction also doesn't work well when misbehavior is self-rewarding. For example, you may be able to keep from grimacing if a youngster kicks you in the shin, but the kid still knows you were hurt—therein lies the reward. In such circumstances, you must discipline the player for the undesirable behavior.

Extinction works best in situations in which players are seeking recognition through mischievous behaviors, clowning, or grandstanding. Usually, if you are patient, their failure to get your attention will cause the behavior to disappear. However, be alert so that you don't extinguish desirable behavior. When youngsters do something well, they expect to be positively reinforced. Not rewarding them will likely cause them to discontinue the desired behavior.

Discipline

Some educators say we should never discipline young people but should only reinforce their positive behaviors. They argue that discipline does not work, creates hostility, and sometimes leads to avoidance behaviors that may be more unwholesome than the original problem behavior. It is true that discipline does not always work and that it can create problems when used ineffectively, but when used appropriately, discipline is effective in eliminating undesirable behaviors without creating undesirable consequences. You must use discipline effectively because it is impossible to guide players through positive reinforcement and extinction alone. Discipline is part of the positive approach when these guidelines are followed:

- Discipline in a corrective way to help players improve now and in the future. Don't discipline to retaliate and make yourself feel better.
- Impose discipline in a matter-of-fact way when players break team rules or otherwise misbehave. Shouting at or scolding children indicates that your attitude is one of revenge.

- Once a good rule has been agreed on, ensure that players who violate it experience the unpleasant consequences of their misbehavior. Warn players once before disciplining, but don't wave discipline threateningly over their heads—just do it.

- Be consistent in administering discipline.

- Don't discipline using consequences that may cause you guilt. If you can't think of an appropriate consequence right away, tell the player you will talk with her after you think about it. You might consider involving a teenage player in designing her own consequence.

- Once the discipline is completed, don't make players feel that they are in the doghouse. Always let them know they're valued members of the team.

- Make sure that what you think is discipline isn't perceived by the player as a positive reinforcement. For instance, keeping a player out of a certain activity or portion of the training session may be just what the child desired.

- Never discipline players for making errors when they are playing.

- Never use physical activity—running laps or doing push-ups—as discipline. To do so only causes players to resent physical activity, whereas we want them to learn to enjoy it throughout their lives.

- Discipline sparingly. Constant discipline and criticism causes players to resent you and to turn their interests elsewhere as well.

Attacking

This chapter focuses on the attacking skills and tactics your players must learn in order to perform effectively in youth soccer games. Remember to use the IDEA approach to teaching skills: Introduce, demonstrate, and explain the skill, and then attend to players as they practice it (see page 76 in chapter 6). This chapter also ties in directly to the season and practice plans in chapter 11. It describes the technical and tactical skills that you'll teach at the training sessions outlined there. If you aren't familiar with soccer skills, rent or purchase a video, such as *Skills School: Developing Essential Soccer Techniques* from US Youth Soccer, so that you can see the skills performed correctly.

Because the information in this book is limited to soccer basics, you will need to advance your coaching knowledge as your players advance their skills. You can do this by learning from your experiences, watching and talking with more experienced coaches, attending coaching courses conducted by your state association, and studying resources on advanced skills.

Attacking Technical Skills

The attacking skills you will teach your players are dribbling, shooting, receiving, passing, and heading. The skills are in priority order. Mastering these techniques will enable your players to better execute your attacking tactics—or set plays—during a match. These basic skills serve as the foundation for playing soccer well at all levels. Soccer players practice these technical skills at every training session, from youth soccer to the pros.

Dribbling

Dribbling is moving and controlling the ball using only the feet. Soccer players dribble to move the ball down the field for a pass or shot, to keep the ball from the opposing team, and to change direction. Some players may have trouble dribbling at first, especially those at younger levels or those who have not played soccer before.

Players need to be able to use the inside and outside of each foot as well as the sole and the instep to dribble (see figure 7.1, *a-d*) while keeping the ball near the body and close to the feet. When dribbling with the inside of the foot (see figure 7.2a), the player turns the foot out and then pushes the ball forward with the arch of the foot. When dribbling with the outside of the foot (see figure 7.2b), the player turns the foot in and then pushes the ball slightly forward or to the side with the arch of the foot.

> **COACHING TIP** Encourage players to use either foot to dribble because this versatility will make it easier for them to protect the ball from opponents. The ability to change speed and direction with either foot will greatly advance a player's skills.

FIGURE 7.1 Parts of the foot used in dribbling: *(a)* inside (arch), *(b)* outside, *(c)* instep, and *(d)* sole.

FIGURE 7.2 Dribbling with the *(a)* inside and *(b)* outside of the foot.

Players should first practice dribbling at a slow pace, such as dribbling while walking. Once they can do so and feel more comfortable with the technique, they can speed up their pace. As your players improve, you can have them dribble against an opponent to help teach them other important aspects of the technique of dribbling, such as varying their speed, changing direction, and shielding the ball. You can also help prepare them for defensive pressure by practicing speeding up and slowing down as they dribble or dribbling around cones or other objects.

Use these points to teach your players how to dribble correctly:

- Push the ball softly in the desired direction, especially if you are dribbling close to defenders.

- Don't constantly watch the ball. Learn to glance up and down at the ball in order to control it and at the same time scan the field. When you are always looking down, an opponent is more likely to be able to steal the ball, or you may not see another teammate who is open for a pass.

- Shield the ball from opponents by positioning your body between the ball and the opponent.

- Move at a speed at which you can control the ball.

It is common for the ball to get away from players at younger levels because their eye–foot coordination, balance, and control of the force they use to touch the ball are not fully developed. A deft touch on the ball comes only with age and years of playing. When the ball gets away, players run the risk of having it stolen by the opponent. To help your players control the ball while dribbling, teach them the following:

- Keep the ball near the body, close to the feet, as shown in figure 7.2.

- Nudge the ball gently in different directions, never letting it get more than a stride's length away.

For the older age groups, preferably U8 and up, intentional speed dribbling—dribbling at a high speed—is acceptable. Speed dribbling is done by pushing the ball out several feet ahead and then sprinting to the ball. When dribbling at high speeds, however, players must keep a close eye out for the opponents and for open teammates. Above all, they must keep their heads up.

For more dribbling practice, see the activity on page 106.

COACHING TIP Players need to spend more time with the ball. From the ages of 6 to 14, ball skills must take precedence over the score and the win–loss record. Without ball skills, dynamic, intelligent, tactical, and exciting soccer in the late teenage years will not be possible.

Shooting

Nothing puts greater pressure on the defense than shots on goal, so your players should become comfortable with the skill of shooting.

A good shot has the same qualities as a good pass—accuracy, proper pace, and timing. So when you first teach the skill of shooting, you may want to point out the similarities. For example, shots also come from the inside, instep, and outside of the foot. Also mention some of these key differences between shooting and passing:

- *Length:* Shots often must travel a greater distance than passes because defenders work to keep offensive players away from the goal.
- *Speed:* Shooters frequently kick the ball harder than passers do so that the keeper can't react to stop the shot. Unlike the passer, the shooter doesn't need to be concerned about whether a teammate can control the ball.
- *Purpose:* Shots are taken for one reason: to score a goal. However, players pass the ball for many different reasons, such as to get a better shot or to keep the ball away from the defense.

COACHING TIP Older or more accurate shooters should aim away from the keeper and toward the corners of the goal. Younger or less accurate shooters can also attempt to hit the corners but might consider using the whole goal as the target at times. Once a goalkeeper becomes part of the game, shooting requires greater accuracy; in order to beat the goalkeeper, the best spot to place a shot is in the corners of the goal.

Use these points to teach your players how to shoot a ball:

- Approach the ball from behind and at a slight angle, with the shoulders and hips square to the target. Keep the head steady and the eyes focused on the ball.
- Take a long step to help draw the kicking leg back, and plant the balance foot beside the ball, with the knee slightly flexed. Keep the kicking leg cocked until the nonkicking foot is firmly planted beside the ball (see figure 7.3a on page 92).
- Extend the kicking foot, keeping the knee of the kicking leg directly over the ball (see figure 7.3b).
- Whip the kicking leg straight, and contact the center of the ball with the instep. Keep the foot firm as it strikes the ball, and keep the toes pointed down (see figure 7.3c).
- Follow through completely, keeping the kicking leg pointing toward the goal well beyond the point of impact (see figure 7.3d).

For more shooting practice, see the activities on pages 107 to 109.

FIGURE 7.3   Shooting the ball.

Receiving

Controlling and redirecting a moving ball all in one motion is called receiving. A player may receive the ball with just about any part of the body—the foot, the thigh, or the chest.

COACHING TIP Correct execution of the skill of receiving is possible for the U10 age group and up. For the U6 age group, coaches should focus on teaching players the mechanics of just stopping the ball. At the U8 age level, coaches can begin teaching players the concept of trapping—stopping the ball while in a stationary position—and can also begin occasionally experimenting with receiving.

Receiving With the Foot

A ball is typically received with the foot when the ball is rolling toward a player. The U8 age group and up, however, can also use the foot to receive a bouncing ball. The U12 age group and up can use the foot to receive a ball in the air. Receiving a ball that is on or near the ground with the inside of the foot provides the most surface area; it is the best method for younger or inexperienced players. Properly receiving a ball on or near the ground, however, is all about knowing how to cushion it. If a player does not cushion the ball, it will bounce away from the foot, and the player will lose control. Use these points to teach players how to receive a ball with the inside of the foot:

- Stand in front of the ball, and extend a leg and foot out to meet it (see figure 7.4a).
- Contact the middle and side of the ball with the inside of the foot, midway between the heel and toes, and cushion the impact of the ball by relaxing the foot as the ball contacts it (see figure 7.4b).
- Pull the leg back to slow the ball (see figure 7.4c).

FIGURE 7.4 Receiving with the inside of the foot.

Players will not always be in a position to receive the ball with the inside of the foot, so they should also learn how to receive with the outside and top of both feet. For example, a player may choose to use the outside of the foot to receive the ball if she is being marked by an opponent because doing so can help shield the ball from the opponent. Receiving with the outside of the foot, as shown in figure 7.5, is the same as receiving with the inside of the foot except the contact surface is smaller. Mistakes, however, may be more likely to occur while players learn the proper touch to control the ball with the outside of the foot. Receiving with the top of the foot, as shown in figure 7.6, requires the player to first accurately judge the flight or bounce of the ball, but the procedure is then the same as for receiving with the inside of the foot.

FIGURE 7.5   Receiving with the outside of the foot.

FIGURE 7.6   Receiving with the top of the foot.

COACHING TIP   Receiving a ball from the air with any part of the foot is a skill best taught to the U12 age group and up. Children generally do not develop enough visual acuity to properly judge the flight of a ball in the air until around age 10, so for the U10 age group and younger, coaches should focus on receiving rolling and bouncing balls.

Receiving With the Thigh

A ball is typically received with the thigh when the ball approaches a player from the air. Use these points to teach your players how to receive a ball with the thigh:

- Stand in front of the ball and flex one knee (see figure 7.7*a*).
- Raise the leg so that the thigh is approximately parallel to the ground and in line with the descent of the ball (see figure 7.7*b*).
- Stop the ball, cushioning it by dropping the knee slightly as the ball touches the midthigh, halfway between the knee and the hip (see figure 7.7*c*).
- As the ball drops to the ground, control the ball by trapping it with the foot (see figure 7.7*d*).

FIGURE 7.7   Receiving with the thigh.

Receiving With the Chest

A ball is typically received with the chest when the ball approaches a player from the air. Use these points to teach your players how to receive a ball with the chest:

- Stand in the ball's line of flight, with arms held up for balance and chest pushed out to meet the ball (see figure 7.8a).
- Allow the ball to make contact just right or left of center chest (see figure 7.8b), where muscle and soft tissue provide an excellent receiving surface.
- As the ball contacts the body, exhale to help relax the controlling surface, and pull the chest back a bit to cushion the ball.
- As the ball drops to the ground (see figure 7.8c), control the ball by trapping it with the foot.

For more practice receiving, refer to the activities on pages 110 to 111.

FIGURE 7.8 Receiving with the chest.

Passing

Passing is the invisible thread that ties teammates together. Passing allows a team to maintain possession of the ball and create scoring opportunities. Passes should be accurate, with appropriate pace, and players should release the ball with proper timing and disguise. Inaccurate or slow passes are likely to be stolen by an opposing player. The length of the pass will vary according to the tactical circumstances, such as where the player with the ball is positioned and where teammates are positioned. Here we will discuss two of the more common types of passes—short and long.

Short Passes

Players use short passes (or push passes) most often because of their accuracy. It is best to use the push pass when the receiver is within 20 yards of the passer. Of course, the passing distance of younger players will be shorter, whereas older players may be able to pass farther on their so-called short passes. Use these points to teach your players how to make a short pass:

- Plant the nonkicking foot alongside and near the ball (see figure 7.9a).
- Square up the hips and shoulders to the receiver, and turn out the kicking foot (see figure 7.9b).
- Swing the kicking foot straight at the center of the ball.
- Follow through by swinging the kicking leg well beyond the point of impact with the ball, in the direction of the receiver (see figure 7.9c).

FIGURE 7.9 Short pass.

Long Passes

Long passes are made when a game situation calls for a player to make a long pass to a teammate across or far down the field. The long pass can be either on the ground or in the air, but it is generally best on the ground for ease of control by the receiver. However, if opponents are between the passer and receiver, the long pass should be made in the air because it is less likely to be intercepted by an opponent. Use these points to teach your players how to make a long pass:

- Plant the nonkicking foot slightly behind and to the side of the ball, with the toes pointing toward the receiver (see figure 7.10a).

- Square up the hips and shoulders to the receiver.

- Point the toes of the kicking foot down, and kick underneath the ball with the top of the foot, at the shoelace or instep area.

- Watch the kicking foot as it contacts the bottom half of the ball (or the middle of the ball for a long pass along the ground) and lifts it off the ground (see figure 7.10b). Keep the kicking foot firm throughout the kicking motion.

- Follow through by swinging the kicking leg slightly up and across the body (see figure 7.10c).

FIGURE 7.10   Long pass.

First-Touch Passes

A first-touch pass can be a long or short pass that a player makes with his first touch of the ball. This pass requires experienced ability to read the movement of the ball in order for the player to get his body into the correct posture to make a pass on the first touch. Players may call on such passes when opponents are tightly marking them or when they are about to receive a ball that is in danger of being taken by an opponent. Passing technique is essentially the same as that described for both the short and long passes, depending on the distance of the pass. This pass is possible in the U8 and U10 age groups, but players in the U12 age group and up are likely to perform it with greater consistency. Coaches of U8 and U10 players do better to teach their youngsters to receive, control, and then pass the ball, using two or three touches of the ball.

A crucially important type of long pass is the cross. Simply put, a cross is a long pass from a flank into the center of the field. Typically, crossing occurs in the attacking third and is used to deliver the ball from the flank into the opposing team's penalty area for a scoring attempt. A cross needs to be accurate, with proper height and pace. Crossing the ball on the move is a difficult skill that takes years of practice to perfect. Players in the U10 age group can begin to work on this skill; it will be refined as the players mature.

For more practice on passing, see the activities on pages 112 to 114.

Heading

Your players can pass or strike at goal using a skill called heading, which is the technique of using the forehead, between the eyebrows and the hairline, to propel and direct the ball.

Heading should be taught beginning with the U12 age group. This restriction is due to the development of visual acuity mentioned earlier in this chapter and the impact this development has on judging the flight of a ball in the air. Heading the ball also requires some upper-body strength, which is just beginning to develop in pubescent children. Let each child learn the skill as his confidence leads him to it. No matter when a player begins to learn the skill, it is vitally important that the coach take the time to teach the skill well. For field players, as well as diving for goalkeepers, heading is a skill that, when done incorrectly, can cause injury. Therefore, coaches must know the techniques of heading well as they begin to teach them to players. When the techniques are taught correctly and thoroughly by coaches, the likelihood of injury from performing the skill is dramatically reduced.

Use these points to teach your players how to head the ball:

- Assume a balanced and relaxed stance with the feet apart. Pull the head and body back, and move to the ball (see figure 7.11*a*).

- Thrust the body forward to meet the ball, hitting it with the forehead at the hairline (see figure 7.11*b*).

- Clench the neck muscles, keeping the neck firm while driving forward (see figure 7.11*c*).

FIGURE 7.11   Heading the ball.

COACHING TIP   When heading the ball, players must keep their eyes on the ball and their mouths closed. Gaping jaws can cause players to bite their tongues.

Heading is often performed incorrectly because coaches often don't know the exact technique involved. Beginner players and coaches can better learn this skill using an underinflated or foam soccer ball to practice individual juggling with the head. This exercise helps players be sure the ball contacts the correct part of the forehead and allows them more practice at judging the movement of the ball in the air.

For more heading practice, see the defending activity on page 133.

Attacking Set Play Techniques

Players need repeated training to master the basic skills of soccer, but they must also learn how to use these skills in match conditions. Some of those conditions are set plays requiring good passing, shooting, and, perhaps, heading skills.

Corner Kick

A corner kick is a direct free kick taken by the attack if the ball goes out of bounds across the goal line when it was last touched by the defense. Corner kicks are taken from the corner arc and are executed most successfully when they are initiated by a kicker who can deliver an accurate pass to either the near-post area or far-post area. For a corner kick, kickers typically use an instep drive, which is a powerful kick made with the top of the foot. The best kicks are hard, low kicks across the face of the goal; these kicks should be in the air, not on the ground. Higher, softer kicks—and kicks on the ground—are easier to defend. Hard, low balls across the face of the goal present more opportunities for the attackers. The mechanics of striking the ball for a corner kick are similar to those of taking a goal kick.

Goal Kick

A goal kick is a placekick made by the defense if the ball goes out of bounds across the goal line when it was last touched by the attack. The goal kick is taken from the goal area. The kicker, usually the goalkeeper, places the plant foot beside the ball (approximately 6 inches to the side), with the toes pointing toward the target and the knee of the standing leg slightly bent. The kicking leg swings back and then forward to strike the ball, with the toes of the kicking foot pointed down, the ankle locked, and the knee slightly bent. The knuckle of the big toe should go under the ball to provide a slight lift to the pass, and the instep should drive through the ball to provide distance to the pass. Players should lean slightly forward when making this kick and keep their eyes on the ball to ensure proper contact. Players should not bring their heads up until the follow-though of the kicking leg is complete.

Penalty Kick

A penalty kick is a direct free kick awarded to the attack when the defense commits a major foul within its own penalty area. For the penalty kick, most shooters try to place the ball in a corner of the goal and use an instep drive or push pass to do so. The instep drive provides the power needed to beat the goalkeeper, and it may be necessary against experienced and faster goalkeepers. The push pass is highly accurate but slower, and a goalkeeper with good reaction speed may be more likely to make the save. Players should also be aware that low shots work best to beat the goalkeeper.

Attacking Tactical Skills

Once your team can understand and properly execute the individual attacking technical skills, they can begin putting them together into attacking game plans, or tactics. The tactics you should teach your players to use when your team has the ball are providing support, moving continuously, spreading out the attack, and improvising in the attacking half of the field.

Providing Support

Essential to any soccer team's attacking success is how players support their teammates on the field. The triangle formation, as shown in figure 7.12, is a way you can reinforce to players in the U10 age group and up the need to provide support to spread out the defense. The triangle formation helps give the player with the ball more options, such as continuing to dribble, making a pass, or shooting on goal if space is opened up by teammates off the ball. It also provides for width and depth, which are other important principles of attack.

The triangle formation is used in sports such as hockey and basketball in which a fluid, dynamic interplay is required. To achieve this formation, players in the immediate vicinity of the ball should work to maintain triangle positioning on the field, with the dribbler usually at the apex of the triangle. In other words, only two or three players should provide support at one time because more will draw too many defenders and clog the attack. Generally players should attempt to maintain a 3- to 5-yard distance from the ball when in close quarters and an 8- to 10-yard distance if defenders are not challenging for possession.

FIGURE 7.12 Triangle formation.

COACHING TIP A simple way to teach the proper triangle formation positioning to players in the U10 age group and up is to position players along the outer edges of the dribbler's field of vision. This outer edge can be found by swinging both arms from behind the back around to the front until they are just visible.

Additionally, coaches of the U12 age group and up should teach players the concept of maintaining a diamond formation in the vicinity of the ball when attacking (see figure 7.13). This shape provides depth and width simultaneously and creates more options for the teammate in possession of the ball.

Coaches should keep in mind that for the U6 age group, the focus should be on creating individual solutions to the game's challenges; therefore, coaches should not introduce the triangle concept at this young age. The U8 age group will also be individually oriented for the most part, but players should be capable of working in pairs.

FIGURE 7.13 Diamond formation.

Wall Passes

The wall pass, or give-and-go, is an advanced support skill in which two attackers can work together to beat a single defender.

To execute the wall pass, the player with the ball dribbles at the defending player, committing the defender to her, then passes to a nearby teammate before sprinting into the space behind the defender to collect a return pass. Note that, to commit a defender to her, the attacker must get the defender to step forward to tackle the ball.

It is the dribbler's responsibility to engage the defender and then to successfully pass to the support attacker. It is the support attacker's responsibility to be about 3 to 4 yards to the side of the defending player, at about a 45-degree angle from the dribbler. The support attacker executes a one-touch pass to the space behind the defender and then sprints forward to support her teammate.

Moving Continuously

Attacking players are easy to mark if they are inactive, so you must encourage your players to move continuously to an open area to receive passes from teammates. The dribbler should keep this principle in mind as well; if other players are not open, he should also strive to move the ball to an open area. This tactic will put pressure on the defense and most likely will cause one of the defending players to leave his player, thus leaving an attacking player open for a pass. However, players should not run merely for the sake of running. Attacking off-the-ball runs need to be for a tactical purpose, such as to support the teammate in possession of the ball, to create space for that player, or for a player to create space for himself. As discussed in the previous section, attackers at the U10 age group and up should also strive to maintain the triangle shape around the ball.

> **COACHING TIP** Though coaches often stress running, it's not necessary for players to run so much. Soccer is played with the brain. A player needs to be in the right place at the right time. You want your players to learn how to run little, and run smart.

Additionally, when a pass is made, the player for whom the pass is intended should move to meet the ball as quickly as possible while still maintaining sufficient control to receive the pass. Players must be aware of the pass, including its direction and velocity, and must pay particular attention to the position of defenders in relation to the path of the pass. Moving to meet the ball makes it less likely that the pass will be intercepted by the opposition.

Spreading Out the Attack

Your players should strive to keep appropriate distances between each other on the field. By spreading your attack, your team can open up space for dribbling, passing, and scoring opportunities. There is no tactical difference between spreading out the attack and providing support, discussed previously on page 102. The players in the diamond or triangle formations are considered support near the vicinity of the ball. When players spread out the attack, however, those farther from the ball also provide support. This concept becomes important for the U12 age group and up, since they will be able to pass the ball farther—the tactical idea of spreading out becomes more real to them. Because of less strength, unrefined technique, and tactical immaturity, the U10 and younger age groups will not play the ball over such large distances; they generally play the game within close vicinity of the ball.

Passing and Shooting Frequently

Quick, frequent passes require the defense to adjust constantly. Also, when defenders are out of position, openings are created for shots on goal. The more shots on goal taken by your players from reasonable distances and angles increases your team's chances to score.

Coaches should keep in mind that the U6 and U8 age groups typically will not pass with intentional forethought or will be inconsistent in their passing. The U10 age group and up will regularly pass on purpose. The older the players, the more often that passing—leading to shots on goal—will occur.

Attacking Activities

The training activities to develop attacking talents in your players are designed to develop not just their ball skills but also their decision making, their physical fitness, and their teamwork. When you coach them during these training activities, focus on their decision making. The soccer brain is the most important part of a soccer player's body to be developed.

American players need to spend more time with the ball. From ages 5 to 14 ball skills must take precedence over the score. These attacking activities put players into game-like situations. The activities will challange them physically and mentally. Players learn more when they are having fun and engrossed with the challenges of proper activities.

➤ CROSSING ON THE DRIBBLE

Goal

- *U6-U10:* To develop dribbling skills
- *U12 and U14:* To warm up

Description   Any number of players can participate in this activity. The playing area is a grid to half of the field depending on the number and ages of the players. The players are split into two teams and stand on opposite touchlines. Each player has a ball. On the word "Go," each player dribbles rapidly to the other touchline. The team whose balls all finish on the opposite line first wins 1 point. Care should be taken that the two opposing teams don't obstruct each other as they cross. Play for 5 to 10 minutes.

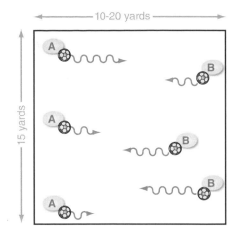

- *U6:* No teams; play as one large group all going in the same direction.
- *U8:* Widen the training area so the teams have more room to maneuver around one another.
- *U10-U14:* Play as described.

Variations

- The higher the skill level of the players, the smaller the playing area can be.
- To make the activity more challenging for older or more skilled players, introduce twists, jumps, hops, and skips into the dribbling routine.

➤ HOT SHOTS

Goal To develop shooting skills

Description Play 4v4, with each team positioned on half of the playing field. A half circle is marked in front of the goal, as shown in the diagram. The game is started by a neutral goal kick made by a player designated by the coach. One team attacks, trying to score goals, while the other defends to avoid conceding them. A goal may be scored only by a shot from outside the half circle. If a player treads within the half circle, the other team is awarded a direct free kick from that spot—no offside or corner kicks. Balls that roll into the shooting circle either go to the goalkeeper (U10-U14) or go back into play with a kick-in (U6 and U8). All balls that go out of bounds are brought back into play with a throw-in (U10-U14) or a kick-in (U6 and U8).

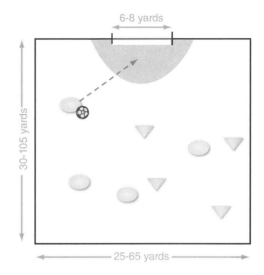

- *U6:* Playing field is 30 yards long by 25 yards wide, with a 6-by-18-yard or smaller goal size; 5-minute playing time.

- *U8:* Playing field is 35 yards long by 30 yards wide, with a 6-by-18-yard or smaller goal size; 5- to 7-minute playing time.

- *U10:* Playing field is 60 yards long by 45 yards wide, with a 6-by-18-yard goal size; 10-minute playing time. Add a neutral goalkeeper.

- *U12:* Playing field is 80 yards long by 55 yards wide, with a 6-by-18-yard goal size; 15-minute playing time. Add a neutral goalkeeper.

- *U14:* Playing field is 105 yards long by 65 yards wide, with an 8-by-24-yard goal size; 15-minute playing time. Add a neutral goalkeeper.

➤ SHOOTING BY NUMBERS

Goal To practice finishing. Secondary goals include practicing dribbling, passing, receiving, and off-the-ball running skills; improving fitness; and developing competitive spirit.

Description Play in teams of 3 to 5 in a playing area 40 yards long by 20 yards wide, with two small goals as shown in the diagram. The players on the teams are numbered consecutively, and each player must score according to this sequence. One team starts the activity by playing the ball between themselves so that their number 1 can score. When number 1 has scored, the team must maneuver number 2 into a goal-scoring position, and so on. The opposing players get a turn if they win the ball, if the ball goes out of play, or if a foul is committed. There are no proper goalkeepers. Play until every player on one team has scored.

- *U6:* Allow the players to score in any sequence. A child may score more than once while the other two players on the team are still trying to score a first time.
- *U8:* Begin with teams of three; later play the activity as described.
- *U10-U14:* Play the activity as described.

Variations

- To make the activity more difficult, limit the number of times the ball can be played.
- Also to make the activity more difficult, indicate which foot or technique can be used for shooting.
- When playing with 5 players, add goalkeepers.

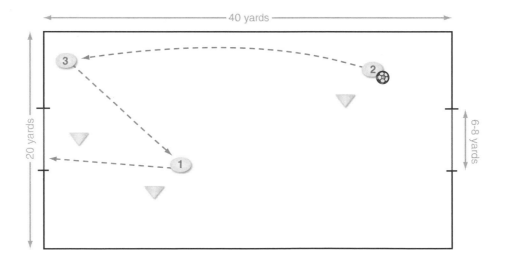

➤ MOBILE GOAL GAME

Goal   To practice quick passing and shooting. Secondary goals include practicing receiving on the move, developing vision of the playing area, and improving group decision making.

Description   Play in teams of 3 to 5 in a playing area measuring 20 yards by 20 yards to 40 yards by 40 yards depending on the age group and the number of players. Both teams play at a mobile goal that is formed by two players, one from each team. They carry a swimming pool noodle in their hands to form the goalposts at either end. This living goal must keep moving around so that as few goals as possible are scored. One team starts the activity in attack. Possession changes after successful tackles or if the ball goes out of play. Play continues directly after each goal with whichever team has the ball. Goals may be scored from either side of the goal. For each period of play, two new players substitute as goalposts. Each player must be a goalpost at least once. Play several intense 5-minute rounds, with breaks to change players. Young players should play shorter rounds.

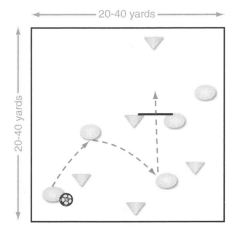

- *U6:* Focus on dribble and then shoot. Only adults should act as the goalposts.
- *U8:* Mostly dribble and then shoot, but occasionally play the activity in pairs to emphasize passing and shooting. Only adults should act as the goalposts.
- *U10-U14:* Play as described.

Variations

- Adults must act as the goalposts when playing this activity with the U6 and U8 age groups.
- To make the activity easier for younger or less skilled players, use more balls to give more players chances to shoot.
- To make the activity more challenging for older or more skilled players, the carriers can reduce the size of the goal.

➤ SOCCER TENNIS

Goal   To practice receiving the ball off the bounce or out of the air. Secondary goals include practicing lofting the ball, striking half-volleys and volleys, and heading and visually tracking a ball in flight.

Description   Play 1v1 up to 5v5 in an area 20 yards long by 10 yards wide, with a net across the middle as shown in the diagram. Playing by tennis rules, the players kick the ball back and forth across the net. Each player tries to reach the ball and return it in such a way that opposing players are unable to retrieve it. Play for 10 to 20 minutes or up to a score of 10 points.

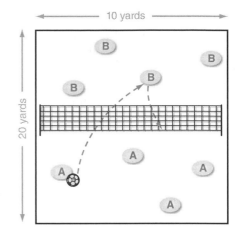

- *U6 and U8:* This activity is not appropriate for these age groups.
- *U10-U14:* Play as described.

Variations

- Play in the gymnasium using a net or a bench.
- Play 1v1 in a small grid.
- To make the activity easier for younger or less skilled players, allow more than one bounce of the ball.
- To make the activity more challenging for older or more skilled players, do not allow any bounce of the ball.

➤ **THIGHS**

Goal   To develop receiving the ball with the thigh

Description   Players divide into pairs and position themselves 5 to 10 yards apart, facing each other. One player (server) tosses the ball underhand to the other player (receiver), who controls the ball with his thigh. The receiver then lets the ball drop to the ground and passes the ball back to the server. The server repeats the underhand toss, and the receiver must use the opposite thigh. Players switch roles after a set number of repetitions. They should remain stationary when starting this activity and progress to receiving with the thigh while on the move.

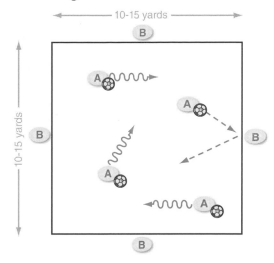

- *U6 and U8:* This activity is not appropriate for these age groups.
- *U10-U14:* Do 10 repetitions (5 with each thigh).

➤ **WINDOWS**

Goal   To practice receiving the ball while turning

Description   Play 4v4, with players positioned on the outside and inside of the playing area, as shown in the diagram. The players on the inside of the area each dribble a ball and pass occasionally to a player on the outside of the area. This outside player must then make a return pass, anywhere in the area, for the player on the inside to receive.

- *U6 and U8:* Play in a 10-by-10-yard playing area; 30-seconds playing time. All passes should be on the ground, and players on the outside can take as many touches as necessary to control the ball and return the pass.

- *U10:* Play in a 15-by-15-yard playing area; 1-minute playing time. Passes should stay on the ground or bounce. Players on the outside play two-touch to control the ball and return the pass.

- *U12 and U14:* Play in a 15-by-15-yard playing area; 2-minute playing time. Passes may be on the ground, bounce, or go in the air. Players on the outside play one-touch return the pass.

➤ PASSING AMONG TEAMS

Goal   To develop passing and receiving

Description   Play 2v2 (U8) or in teams of 3 to 8 (U10-U14) in the penalty area for the age group. Adjust the size of the playing area to the players' capabilities. The smaller the area, the more difficult it is to pass the ball among team members. Both teams have their own ball, each marked differently. Each player passes the ball accurately to his teammate. Points are lost if a player passes to a member of the other team or if the ball goes out of play. For players at the U10 level and above, points are also lost if the ball is passed directly back to the previous player without a third player having touched it. Passes should instead be strung throughout the whole group; after each mistake, the sequence is restarted from the point where the error occurred. Two umpires are needed for this activity to follow each of the balls and to keep score of the points. Play for 20 minutes maximum.

- *U6:* This activity is not appropriate for this age group.
- *U8-U14:* Play as described.

Variation   Limit the number of touches to make the activity more difficult.

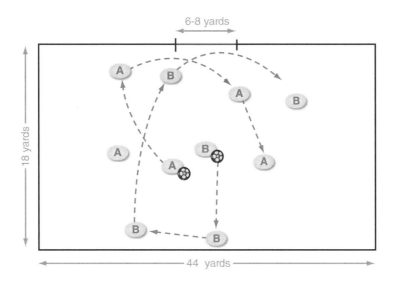

> ## MIDFIELD BUILDUP

Goal   To practice combination passing. Secondary goals include developing group attacking shape, finishing, and improving stamina.

Description   Play 4v4 in a playing area 30 yards long by 20 yards wide, with two small goals on the sidelines, the goalmouths facing outward from the field. Two players on one team must work the ball out of their own half into an attacking position before passing the ball to a teammate positioned in front of the opposing goal; she in turn is marked by one of the opposition. If the ball is lost, the other team continues the activity by attacking. A goal can be scored only after a pass from within the opposing half. The two in-field players may not cross the boundary lines. Passes from within that team's own half are faults and are penalized by a free kick. The two midfield players switch with those standing in front of the goals every 5 minutes. Play for a maximum of 10 5-minute rounds, with 30-second to 1-minute breaks between rounds.

- *U6:* This activity is inappropriate for this age group.
- *U8:* Allow more leeway with this age group when enforcing playing within the boundaries.
- *U10-U14:* Play the activity as described.

Variations

- The length of the field, length of rounds, or number of passes allowed can be altered to suit the capabilities of the players.
- Change midfield players after each goal scored.

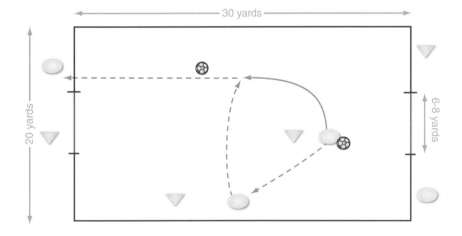

➤ MIDFIELD PENETRATION

Goal To practice passing for penetration. Secondary goals include practicing receiving skills, developing group attacking shape, and improving stamina.

Description Play 5v5 in a playing area 30 yards long by 20 yards wide, with goal areas, two goals on the end line, and thirds of the field marked off, as shown in the diagram. The teams are set up with 2 players in the defending third, 2 players in the midfield third, and 1 player in the attacking third. The activity begins with the defenders in possession of the ball in their defending third. They evade the one opponent and pass the ball out to their teammates in midfield. Here they play 2v2, and the 2 players in midfield win a point if they succeed in reaching their own player in the attacking third with a pass. They receive an additional point for a goal. If the other side wins the ball, play continues without a break. Play for a maximum of six 5-minute rounds, with 30-second to 1-minute breaks between rounds.

- *U6-U8:* This activity is inappropriate for these age groups.
- *U10-U14:* Play the activity as described.

Variations

- Change the midfield players every 5 minutes.
- A point may also be awarded if the attacking player is able to return the ball to midfield.
- The game is simplified if one defender is removed.

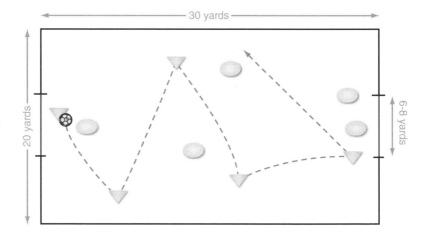

➤ THROW-IN AT OPPOSITION

Goal To develop throw-in skills. Secondary goals include developing strategic thinking as well as improving communication, awareness, and fitness.

Description Play in teams of 6 to 8 in a playing area 20 yards long by 10 yards wide, divided into halves by a center line as shown in the diagram. Teams line up in their own halves but with one player positioned behind the opponents' goal line. The team in possession tries to hit their opponents with the ball in the legs by passing the ball about, using throw-ins. Players who have been hit retire behind the opponents' goal

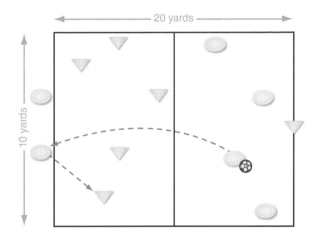

line. These players can throw the ball at their opponents at any time, and if their shot is good they may return to midfield. Those players in the field of play may aim a shot only if they catch the ball in their half. Ball possession changes if the ball can be caught by the player being targeted. The winner is declared when all the members of one team have been hit. Play for 20 minutes maximum.

- *U6 and U8:* This activity is not applicable to these groups since no throw-ins are performed in their games.
- *U10-U14:* Play the activity as described.

Variations
- To train for the long throw, increase the size of the playing area.
- To strengthen the upper body, use a size 5 ball for U10 and U12 players, and use a basketball for U14 and older players.

➤ PARALLEL FOUR-GOAL GAME

Goal To improve peripheral vision. Secondary goals include creating goal-scoring opportunities, switching the point of attack, improving group attacking shape, developing a full range of ball skills, and getting into match shape.

Description Play in teams of 6 to 11 on a normal age-appropriate field used sideways, with two goals on either side. Mark off the field with a halfway line as shown in the diagram. One team attacks either of its opponent's two goals and defends its own goals. A goal is scored when the ball crosses either of the goal lines. Ball possession changes after goals, fouls, and fair tackles and when the ball goes out of play. There is no kickoff from the center; the ball is reintroduced into play by a goal kick. Play for 45 minutes maximum.

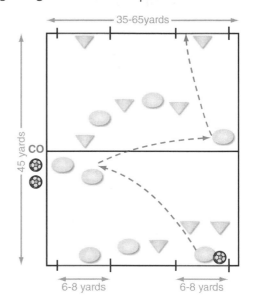

- *U6 and U8:* This activity is not appropriate for these age groups.
- *U10-U14:* Play the activity as described.

Variations

- Two full teams take part, with the final defenders (those closest to the goals) permitted to handle the ball.
- Use two proper goalkeepers.

➤ WINGERS

Goal To develop crossing on the move. A secondary goal is to improve attacking skills, including the group attacking shape, off-the-ball run timing, and finishing.

Description Play in teams of 7 to 11 on a full field. Place additional goals 6 yards wide at the sides, 20 to 25 yards from the goal lines, as shown in the diagram. The attacking team must play the ball through one of the outer goals before taking a shot at the normal goal. The width of the outer goals should depend on the players' skills. The better the players, the narrower these goals should be. Only goals scored in the outer goals count. This can be done in two ways: Either a player can dribble the ball through the outer goal, or the ball can be passed through and then taken on by another attacker. Play for 40 minutes maximum.

- *U6 and U8:* This activity is not appropriate for this age group.
- *U10:* This is a difficult activity for this age group, so the focus should be mostly on the technique of crossing the ball, predominantly to the near-post area.
- *U12 and U14:* Play as described.

Variation Teams of fewer than 7 can play across half the field. Outer goals should be placed accordingly.

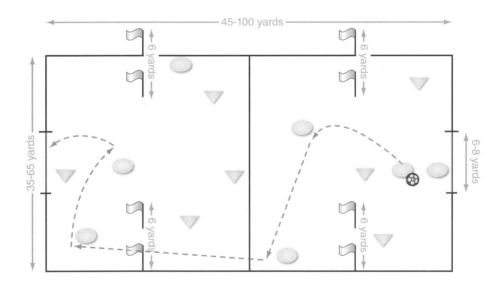

➤ CORNER GOALS GAME

Goal To practice switching the point of attack. Secondary goals include practicing repeated dynamic game situations, combination passing, tactical awareness, principles of attack, group communication, teamwork, and transition, and getting into match shape.

Description Play in teams of 4 to 7 on half of an age-appropriate field, with a goal at each corner consisting of two corner flag posts or tall cones about 2 yards apart, as shown in the diagram. Each team has two goals to defend and the two goals of the opposing team to attack. Since the goals are in the corners, the area is more fully utilized, with the players having to run farther than they have to normally. One team starts the game in its own half and can attack either of the opponent's two goals, depending on the situation. There are no goalkeepers, and ball handling is not permitted. The play changes direction if the opposition wins the ball, if the ball goes out of play, and when a goal is scored. Play for an hour maximum, with appropriate water breaks.

- *U6:* Modify the activity for this age group by allowing the children to score at any of the four goals, the only rule being that they may not score at the same goal twice in a row.
- *U8-U14:* Play the activity as described.

Variations

- Because no goalkeeper is designated in this game, the last player before the goal may handle the ball, using her hands to make a save. Note that this variation does not apply to the U6 and U8 age groups.
- Teams of 7 or more players should use the whole field.

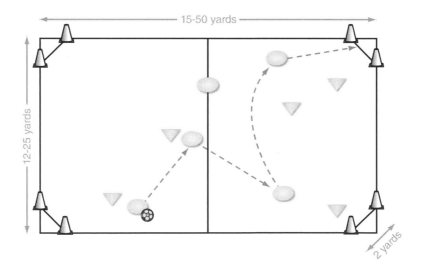

➤ ALL UP IN ATTACK

Goal   To improve compactness (group tactics). Secondary goals include practicing combination passing, receiving, dribbling, shielding, shooting, developing game-related fitness, communication skills, and mental concentration; and game awareness.

Description   Play in teams of 3 to 6 on one half of the field, with a halfway line marked and two small goals, as shown in the diagram. One team attacks, and the other team defends, trying to win the ball. A goal counts only when all attacking players are in the opposition's half. The other side is given the ball if this is not the case when a shot is taken on goal, after interceptions and fouls, and if the ball goes out of play. There are no goalkeepers and no offside rule. Play for 10 minutes up to the equivalent of half a match.

- *U6 and U8:* Perform the activity as described.
- *U10-U14:* Perform the activity as described. At this level, the coach can discuss the need for support on the attack.

Variations

- Teams of more than 7 should use an age-appropriate full-size field.
- If goalkeepers (U10 to U14 age groups) are used, they alone may remain in their own half throughout.

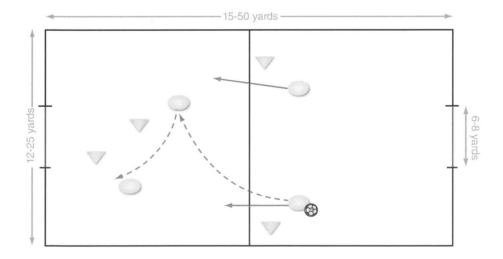

➤ TWO-BALL GAME

Goal To improve mobility. Secondary goals include improving attacking shape, ball skills, peripheral vision, and teamwork.

Description Play in teams of 5 to 7 in a playing area one-third to one-half of a normal age-appropriate field, without goals. One team starts with both balls and must retain possession of the two balls for 1 minute in order to score 1 point. The other team tries to tackle and harass the team in possession. After time is up, the activity continues until one ball is lost. The opponents then receive the other ball and start their 2-minute period. A team loses both balls if a player commits a foul or a ball goes out of play. Two referees (coaches or parents) should be used, one following each ball. Play for 30 minutes maximum.

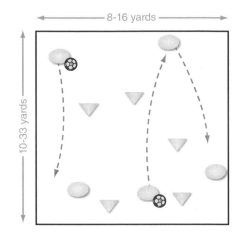

- *U6:* Play in teams of 3, focusing on dribbling and shooting skills.
- *U8:* Play in teams of 4, focusing on mobility in order to support the teammate with the ball.
- *U10-U14:* Play the activity as described.

Variations

- Vary the time that both balls must be kept to suit the level of the players' skill (1 to 3 minutes).
- Award points not on a time basis but according to the errors committed. Ball possession changes after each error.
- Teams of more than 7 players should play on two-thirds of the field.

Defending

8

Playing

Playing defense consists largely of instinct and effort, but training and repetition will help improve your players' defensive techniques and tactics. This chapter focuses on the defending techniques and tactics that your players must learn to succeed in youth soccer.

Defending Technical Skills

The five defending technical skills your players need to learn are marking, tackling, heading, intercepting passes, and making clearances.

Marking

Marking is the skill of guarding attacking players to prevent them from scoring. A defender uses this skill to slow down an opponent and to allow teammates to recover to their positions. Marking is a good example of the link between technique and tactics. Selecting whom to mark (and when, where, and for how long) is primarily a player's tactical decision. From a technical viewpoint, however, marking an opponent well requires correct physical positioning and posture.

> **COACHING TIP** Teach players in the U10 age group and up to pay close attention to an opponent's habits, such as using only one foot to dribble, pass, or shoot. Then, if these habits occur during the flow of play, attentive players will be able to outwit the attacking opponents and perhaps block or gain possession of the ball more frequently.

Defenders should try to mark the attacking player nearest them by positioning themselves between that player and the goal, which is called being goalside. For example, in figure 8.1, player 1 is goalside of player 2. From this position, defending players are better able to gain possession of the ball off the dribble and to intercept passes. Also, the closer a defender is to the player with the ball, the more difficult it is for that player to pass, dribble, or shoot. Marking gives defending players a better chance of stealing or blocking the ball when the opponent passes or shoots.

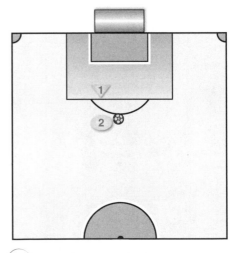

FIGURE 8.1 Goalside positioning.

Use these points when coaching your players on how to mark:

- Maintain ready position, with feet approximately shoulder-width apart, knees bent, and body leaning slightly forward. The head should be steady and the arms slightly out to help maintain balance.

- Eyes should be focused on the ball and on the dribbler's hips.
- Adjust positioning based on the dribbler's speed, ability, and location on the field (see figure 8.2).

For more marking practice, see the activity on page 130.

FIGURE 8.2   Marking.

Tackling

Taking the ball from an attacker is called tackling. The primary intent of tackling is for the tackler to gain possession of the ball. To simply kick the ball away from the dribbler may dispossess the attacker but does not gain possession for the tackler. Effective tackling is all about timing. Ideally, your players should step in whenever the attacker temporarily loses control of the ball. Players should not be afraid to attempt to take the ball when they have a good opportunity, such as when the dribbler pushes the ball too far ahead or when a player does not receive a pass correctly.

COACHING TIP The defender should not always simply wait for the dribbler to make a move and then react to it. Instead, the defender can use her own feints to make the dribbler think she is overcommitted so the dribbler will go in a predictable direction. Then, the defender is ready to step in and take the ball.

Lunging at the ball—also called diving in—is a poor tactic for gaining possession, and a good dribbler usually goes around a defender who does so, with no trouble. Also, the rules require the tackler to contact the ball before the opponent and to intentionally play the ball—not rush the opponent, which would be an unfair charge and warrants a foul. When positioning to make a tackle, the defender should instead approach the dribbler in a sideways position and should go for the ball, not the dribbler (see figure 8.3 on page 124). If the defender follows this technique, the attacker cannot push the ball between the defender's legs (called a nutmeg). Defenders should also, however, be prepared to reestablish a good defensive position if they are unsuccessful in their tackling attempts.

Your players can use two types of tackles depending on the situation they are in. These are the block tackle and the poke tackle.

FIGURE 8.3   Approaching the tackle in a sideways position.

Block Tackle for Possession

Your players will want to use a block tackle when an opponent is dribbling directly at them because the tactical objective is to gain possession of the ball for the tackler's team. The block is the most common type of tackle in soccer, and this technique is the foundation of skillful defending.

Use the following points to teach your players how to block tackle:

- Quickly close the distance between yourself and the dribbler.
- Assume a slightly crouched position, with the feet in a staggered stance in order to react more quickly to the dribbler's move (see figure 8.4a).
- To make the tackle, position the foot sideways, making contact with the inside surface of the foot. The foot must be kept firm as it drives into the ball (see figure 8.4b).

Poke Tackle for Dispossession

Your players can use a poke tackle when they are approaching an opponent from the side or from slightly behind. Whereas the block tackle is used for the primary intent of tackling, to gain possession, the poke tackle is used to achieve the secondary intent of tackling, which is to dispossess the opponent.

Use the following points to teach your players how to poke tackle:

- Mark the dribbler as previously specified, and watch for an opportunity to attack the ball.
- Move near the dribbler, and plant the nonkicking foot away from the ball (see figure 8.5a).

FIGURE 8.4 Block tackle.

FIGURE 8.5 Poke tackle.

- With the toes of the other foot, use a short, firm kick near the center of the ball to knock it away from the opponent (see figure 8.5b).

For additional tackling practice, see the activities on pages 131 to 132.

Heading

When defending, players use the skill of heading to clear the ball away from scoring range of the goal. The need to head the ball usually arises from a crossed ball or the opposing goalkeeper's punt. The technical aspects of heading the ball, however, are basically the same whether attacking or defending, except that players defending should strike the ball on the bottom half in order to send it high over attackers. The primary goal of heading to clear the ball when defending is to get the ball away from the danger zone (see figure 8.6).

For additional heading practice, see the activity on page 133.

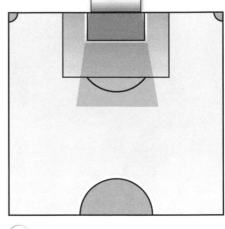

FIGURE 8.6   Danger zone.

Intercepting Passes

Players on the defending team should try to intercept a pass whenever possible rather than wait for an attacker to receive it. Starting a counterattack off an intercepted pass is much easier than starting it after a tackle or after regaining possession from a ball played out of bounds. Defenders need to be alert for opportunities to intercept passes. Intercepting, which is stepping in between the receiver and the ball before the receiver can get it, requires good timing. The best time to intercept a pass is when the receiver is stationary and the pass is slow.

Following are cues for defenders to ask themselves when looking for the best interception opportunities. If the answers are yes to all, then the opportunity is probably a good one.

- Are the receiver's feet flat?
- Is the receiver not moving to the pass or moving slowly?
- Is the receiver looking only at the ball, not aware of defenders around him?

The mechanics of intercepting the ball are the same as those of receiving it. The defender who intercepts the ball then becomes the receiver.

For practice intercepting passes, see the activity on page 134.

Making Clearances

When the attack plays a ball into the danger zone, the defense has a chance of clearing it—meaning they can send the ball high, wide, and far away from the goal. It is preferable, however, for the defense to intercept or tackle for possession. A counterattack is possible once the defense has gained possession by passing, shooting, or dribbling. As defenders become more skillful, many will learn how to turn a clearance into an outlet pass for their team.

For practice making clearances, see the activity on page 135.

Defending Set Play Techniques

Defending techniques, like attacking ones, require players to utilize the basic soccer skills they have learned. However, they must not only know how to perform specific kicking techniques, they must also learn how to successfully defend against these kicks. Training to defend at set plays teaches them how to defend not only as individual players but also as a team.

Corner Kick

Corner kicks can be defended against either by using a zone defense, with the focus on the near-post and far-post areas, or by marking man to man. You can also combine the two, assigning some players to cover the post areas and others to mark individual attackers.

The defending field players must turn their hips one quarter turn outward toward the field of play. With this body posture they can see the ball and attacking runs, and they can be in a better position to clear the ball upfield. Being able to clear the ball is of utmost importance to defending field players. They will most likely do so with the head, since most corner kicks are delivered in the air.

Free Kick (Direct or Indirect)

When defending against a free kick, field players may set up a wall depending on the goalkeeper's needs, the distance between the ball and the goal, and the angle of the ball's path to the goal. The closer the ball is to the danger zone, as shown in figure 8.6, the more players will be needed in the wall. Generally, forwards and midfielders should go into the wall, and fullbacks should be free for zone or man-to-man marking.

Goal Kick

When defending against a goal kick, it is best for the defending team simply to assume their normal team positions. If the opponent taking the goal kick places the ball on one side of the goal area, the defending team may want to shift more players to that side of the field to challenge for the ball once it has cleared the penalty area.

Penalty Kick

When defending against a penalty kick, defending players may go into the penalty area once the ball is kicked, so they must be ready to defend. Defending players should also be ready to enter the penalty area in case the goalkeeper blocks the ball but is unable to hold it, or in case the ball rebounds off the goal. As the defenders enter the penalty area, the skill they are most likely to use is clearing the ball.

Throw-In

When the attacking team has a throw-in in your half of the field, it is a good idea to mark man to man within a 30-yard arc of the point from which the ball is being thrown in. This tactic increases the possibility of a turnover in favor of the defending team.

Defending Tactical Skills

Proper defending is the springboard to the attack. If your team defends skillfully and intelligently, your players are more likely to regain possession of the ball. The defending tactical skills you should teach your players are pressure, cover, recovery, and depth.

Pressure

Pressure is necessary to prevent the opponent who is in possession of the ball from shooting, dribbling, or passing straight at your goal. The defender nearest the opponent in possession of the ball applies the pressure. To truly apply pressure, the defender must be near enough to the attacker so that the latter is concerned that the defender might actually be able to get the ball. Typically, the defender must be within two strides of the attacker.

The good news is that U6 and U8 players tend to apply pressure naturally, by all clustering around the ball simultaneously. From the U10 age group and up, however, one player at a time should apply the pressure. As mentioned before, this player is simply the defender closest to the ball; the position she plays in the team formation is immaterial. Pressure is applied by proper marking of the attackers, especially the one in possession of the ball.

Cover

While one player pressures the opponent with the ball, other defenders in the immediate vicinity of the ball should provide cover. One or two players should provide cover by positioning themselves behind (goalside of) the teammate pressuring the opponent in possession of the ball. This tactic will slow down the opponent's attack and buy time for the rest of the defending team to recover into good defending positions.

All players on the team must help defend. The other players on the defending team should get into team positions to cover the rest of the field in case passes are made by the attacking team. When the ball moves, the players switch roles without switching positions, so defending players may have to pressure or cover depending on where the ball moves.

> **COACHING TIP** Good defending is mostly in the head and heart; it takes clear thinking and commitment. Coaches need to praise young players more often when they defend well; they need to believe that their coach sees and appreciates good defending as much as scoring goals.

Recovery

As soon as possession of the ball is lost to the other team, all players on your team become defenders. One player should apply pressure to the ball to slow down the opposing team's attack. This maneuver buys time for teammates to make recovery runs into good defensive goalside positions or into positions that provide cover for the teammate pressuring the ball. Once teammates have made recovery runs to give cover, the defender pressuring the ball can attempt a tackle. To make good recovery runs into defensive positions, your players must have high levels of self-discipline, fitness, and tactical awareness.

Depth

Depth is the tactical concept of getting into a goalside position between the ball and your goal line. Once defending players have made recovery runs to goalside positions, they should provide depth to the defense by getting into positions across the field, behind the teammates applying pressure or giving cover. If one defender is beaten on the dribble by the attacker with the ball or by a pass or a shot, the other defenders behind still have a chance at the ball. Thus, if the player in possession eludes his defender, the covering defender is on hand to resume the pressure; if the attacker passes, covering defenders are in position to intercept or immediately mark the receiver.

Defending Activities

The activities you will find here for defending build the critical base of teamwork. It is intelligent and skillful defending that is the foundation of team success. Improving your players' skills at defending in turn becomes the springboard of your attack.

➤ MARKING MAN

Goal   To develop marking skills

Description   Players divide into two teams and position in a playing area, divided by a halfway line and with goals set up at each end, as shown in the diagram. No goalkeepers are used. Each defender is assigned a specific opponent to mark, which is known as man-to-man marking. The offense attempts to score while the defense attempts to prevent goals by using effective marking. The game starts when the defense passes the ball across the halfway line to the offense. Defenders may tackle only their own mark; help from teammates is not allowed. The attackers keep the ball if they beat the player marking them in the tackle, after a goal, after fouls, or if the ball goes out of bounds. No player may cross the halfway line.

- **U6:** This activity is not appropriate for this age group.
- **U8:** Play 3v3 or 4v4 in a 20-by-15-yard playing area with 6-yard-wide goals; 10-minute playing time.
- **U10:** Play 4v4 in a 30-by-20-yard playing area with 8-yard-wide goals; 10- to 15-minute playing time.
- **U12:** Play 4v4, 5v5, or 6v6 in a 30-by-20-yard to 40-by-30-yard playing area with 8-yard-wide goals; 15-minute playing time.
- **U14:** Play 5v5, 6v6, or 7v7 in a 40-by-30-yard to 50-by-40-yard playing area with 8-yard-wide goals; 20-minute playing time.

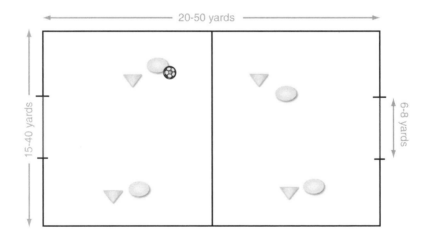

➤ TWO AGAINST TWO IN THE CORNER

Goal   To develop tackling skills. Secondary goals include intercepting passes, as well as stamina.

Description   Play 4v4 in a corner of the field, about 15 by 15 yards. Only two players from each team are allowed on the field at any time. Players are changed at 1-minute intervals. Start the activity with a drop ball by the coach or a game of draw. The skill lies in building up an attacking position that enables the ball to be easily controlled and taken over the opposing team's goal line. A point is scored each time the ball is *dribbled* over the line. The winner is the team with the most points after a given length of time. This activity is particularly suitable for more proficient players.

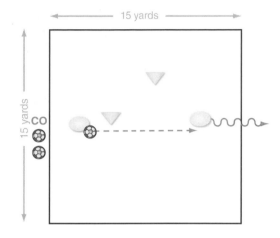

- **U6:** This activity is not appropriate for this age group.
- **U8:** This activity can be played at this age group, but it will be quite complex for them, so be patient.
- **U10-U14:** Play the activity as described.

Variation   Shorten or lengthen the time on and off the field depending on the players' capabilities.

➤ DOUBLE ZONE

Goal   To develop tackling skills

Description   Players divide into two teams and position in a playing area with 3-yard-wide goals set up on the goal line (corner flags or tall cones can be used), as shown in the diagram. Each team has both attackers and defenders. The attackers try to score goals, and the defenders try to stop them. For both teams, attackers are positioned in the opposing half of the playing area, and defenders are positioned in their own half. The coach should have all the balls just off the field at the point where the halfway line meets the touchline. The game starts with a kick-in from the coach, who may also put a spare ball into play as needed. No player may cross over the halfway line. If the defense wins the ball from the attackers, if the ball goes out of play, or if there is an infringement of the rules, the other attackers get the ball. Attackers and defenders must change positions at regular intervals.

- **U6:** This activity is not appropriate for this age group.
- **U8:** Play 4v4 (3 attackers and 1 defender) in a 25-by-15-yard playing area; 10-minute playing time.
- **U10 and U12:** Play 5v5 (3 attackers and 2 defenders) in a 40-by-20-yard playing area; 15-minute playing time.
- **U14:** Play 5v5 (3 attackers and 2 defenders) in a 50-by-30-yard playing area; 20-minute playing time.

Variation   To make the activity more challenging for defenders in the U10 to U14 age groups, allow 1 or 2 more attackers so that the attack has an advantage in numbers.

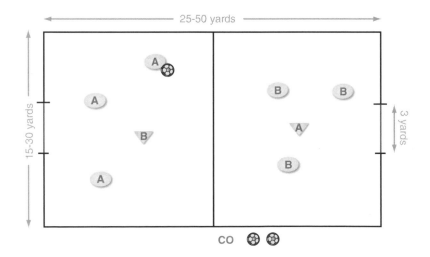

> ### HEADING UP

Goal   To develop defensive heading skills

Description   Play 3v3, with each team positioned anywhere in half of a 20-by-15-yard playing area, as shown in the diagram. Players may move anywhere in their half at any time. One team begins with one player heading the ball into the other half from behind the halfway line. The players on the other team attempt to catch the ball in the air. If the ball is caught, the catcher may take one step forward and head the ball back. Otherwise, the ball is headed from the spot where it lands. The teams continue to head the ball, attempting to force their opponents back and move themselves forward. Direct returns are allowed. If the ball goes out of bounds, the game is resumed with a throw-in, and the ball should be headed from the throw-in.

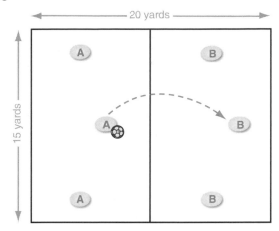

- **U6-U10:** This activity is not appropriate for these age groups.
- **U12 and U14:** Play as described.

Variation   Players at the U14 level may challenge the defending header with an attacking header to shoot at the goal or pass to a teammate.

➤ INTERCEPTION

Goal To develop pass interception skills

Description Players divide into two teams and position in a playing area as shown in the diagram. One neutral player, also positioned in the playing area, starts play by passing to a player on either team. The player who receives the ball passes to another teammate, and the team makes passes among themselves. The opposing team looks for opportunities to block or steal passes, earning a point for each interception. If a pass is made to the neutral player or if the neutral player makes an interception, he can then make a pass to either team. All balls that go out of bounds are brought back into play with a kick-in (U6 and U8) or a throw-in (U10 to U14).

- **U6:** Play 2v2 in a 20-by-20-yard playing area; 5-minute playing time.
- **U8 and U10:** Play 3v3 in a 25-by-35-yard playing area; play to 2 or 3 points; 10-minute playing time.
- **U12 and U14:** Play 4v4 in a 35-by-40-yard playing area; play to 3 or 4 points; 15-minute playing time.

Variations

- To make the activity easier, remove the neutral player and play with even numbers.
- To make the activity more difficult, add a second neutral player.

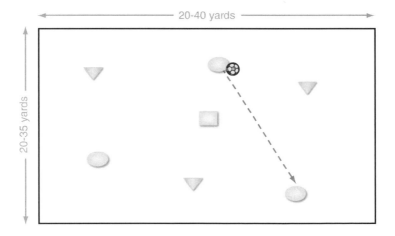

> ### NEUTRAL ZONE

Goal   To develop ball-clearing skills

Description   Players divide into two teams and position in a playing area as shown in the diagram, with two neutral players stationed in zones on either side of the playing area. The two teams must remain in the center area, and only neutral players are allowed in the zones. Players in the center area play a normal soccer match and use defensive clearances with the foot to clear the ball into one of the neutral zones. Neutral players are used to help create good crosses, and a goal may be scored only after a neutral player has crossed the ball.

- **U6:** This activity is not appropriate for this age group.
- **U8 and U10:** Play 4v4 on a 40-by-20-yard playing area; 10-minute playing time.
- **U12 and U14:** Play 6v6 on a 50-by-30-yard playing area; 15-minute playing time.

Variation   To add incentive to the activity, grant a point to the team that makes a clearance meeting all the preferred qualities: high, wide, and long.

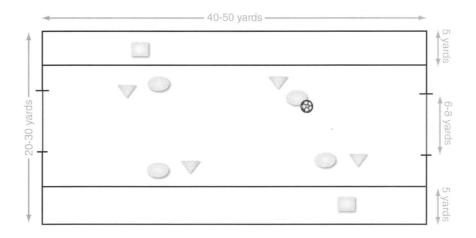

➤ HANDICAP FOOTBALL

Goal To practice tackling skills and intercepting passes. Secondary goals include developing support, learning group tactics and principles of play, and improving stamina.

Description Play 5v3 in a 30-square-yard area. One team passes the ball around, and the opponents try to regain possession of it as quickly as possible. A tackle or an intercepted pass scores 1 point. The team of 5 players has a handicap—first-time passing—whereas the team of 3 is allowed all legal means. The team of 5 earns a point by making five uninterrupted passes. When one team earns a point, the players can opt either to continue or to give the ball to the other side. The winner is the team with the most points after a given time. Adapt the activity to the age and capabilities of the players. Play a maximum of six 5-minute rounds, with short intervals between rounds.

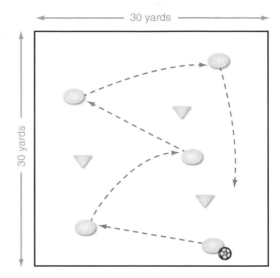

- **U6:** This activity is not appropriate for this age group.
- **U8:** Play with one team of 3 and one team of 2.
- **U10-U14:** Play as described.

Variations
- The team of 5 is allowed only along-the-ground passing, or only left-footed passing, and so on.
- After 5 minutes, the players change roles.

➤ TWO OPEN GOALS

Goal   To improve partner cooperation. Secondary goals include improving shielding, dribbling, passing, receiving, and tackling skills, as well as the ability to intercept passes; developing soccer fitness, communication between teammates, and mental focus; and enhancing overall competition and transition skills.

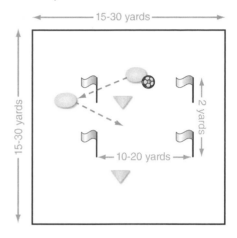

Description   Play in teams of 2 to 4 in a 15-square-yard to 30-square-yard area depending on the number of players and the age group, with flag posts making two goals, each 2 yards wide, as shown in the diagram. There are no goalkeepers. The distance between the goals is 10 to 20 yards. One team attacks and tries to score goals, and the other team defends while trying to win the ball. Since both goals are open, there should be very few interruptions to the game. Both teams are forced to keep running. A goal can be scored from either side of the flag posts. The height of these posts determines the goal (i.e., balls passing above that height are disallowed). Throw-ins (for U10 and older) are taken from the boundary lines. Handling is not allowed, and players cannot run between the flag posts. These fouls are penalized by a free kick from 10 yards out. Play for 20 minutes maximum.

- **U6:** Each player should have a ball. Run the activity focusing on individual ability to shoot from the dribble.
- **U8-U14:** Play as described. The grid should be 15 × 15 for U8, 20 × 20 for U10, 25 × 25 for U12, and 30 × 30 for U14.

Variations

- To make the activity easier for younger or less skilled players, increase the width of the goal to 3 yards.
- To make the activity more challenging for older or more skilled players, decrease the width of the goal to 1 yard.
- Have fewer players for highly skilled groups, more players for those with below-average skills.

Goalkeeping

9

As the last line of defense to prevent a goal, the goalkeeper has the greatest individual defensive responsibility on the team. US Youth Soccer recommends that the position of goalkeeper be introduced in the U10 age group. In the U10 and U12 age groups, the players learning this position will act predominantly as shot stoppers in goal. As they learn the techniques and tactics of the position from the U14 age group and up, they will evolve into goalkeepers.

COACHING TIP Although the goalkeeper isn't introduced into the game until the U10 age group, players from the U6 to the U14 age groups should be exposed to playing all positions on a soccer team, including the goalkeeper for U10 age groups and up.

Goalkeeping Technical Skills

The goalkeeper must be alert and watch the ball at all times. Given the physical demands of the position, the goalkeeper must be one of the best athletes on the team. She should be agile and quick, with strong and sure hands, and also must be willing to speak up to organize the team when defending. As with all soccer players, the most important part of the body is the brain, so always focus on developing thinking players. Yet keep in mind that good footwork allows the hands to find the ball, so never neglect footwork training with goalkeepers.

The following skills are unique to the position of goalkeeper.

Ready Position

When an opponent has the ball within shooting distance of the goal, the goalkeeper must first assume the ready position. The feet are approximately shoulder-width apart, the knees are bent, and the body leans slightly forward. The hands are above waist level, with palms facing forward and fingers pointing upward. The head is steady, and the eyes are focused on the ball (see figure 9.1).

Once an opponent is getting into position to shoot, goalkeepers should maintain their ready position but should come off the goal line toward the ball in an effort to narrow the

FIGURE 9.1 Ready position for goalkeepers.

shooting angle. This maneuver cuts down the amount of goalmouth that is accessible to the shooter. When the keeper comes off the goal line and moves toward the shooter, the shooter's view of the goalmouth will narrow; therefore, it will be harder for the shooter to get a shot on goal. The trade-off is that in narrowing the angle to the goal, the keeper must be able to react more quickly to a shot because the shooter takes it from a closer range to the keeper.

Stopping Shots

The technique to shot stopping, or catching the ball, varies depending on the type of shot made. Shots can be on the ground, at waist height, at chest height, or lofted.

COACHING TIP   When keepers are learning to catch balls shot straight at them, the progression is rolling, bouncing, and then in the air.

Ground Shots

In ground shots, the ball rolls along the ground or just a few inches off the ground. Use the following points to teach your goalkeepers how to stop a ground shot:

- From the ready position, quickly shuffle sideways to a position between the ball and the goal.
- Bend the legs slightly, with the feet approximately shoulder width apart, and bend forward at the waist as the ball arrives (see figure 9.2*a*).
- Extend the arms down, with palms facing forward and hands slightly cupped, and allow the ball to roll up onto the wrists and forearms (see figure 9.2*b*).
- Return to an upright position, clutching the ball tightly to the chest (see figure 9.2*c*).

FIGURE 9.2   Stopping a ground shot.

Shots at Waist Height

Waist-high shots take a path toward the goalkeeper's midsection. Use the following points to teach your goalkeepers how to stop a shot at waist height:

- From the ready position, bend forward at the waist as the ball arrives and extend the arms down, palms facing forward and hands slightly cupped (see figure 9.3a).
- Receive the ball on the wrists and forearms, secure it against the chest, and slide the feet backward a few inches to absorb the impact (see figure 9.3b).

Shots at Chest Height

For shots that take a chest-high path, players must use a different grip, called the W-grip (see figure 9.4a), to allow the fingers to cover more surface area of the ball. Younger players with smaller hands can also use the diamond grip (see figure 9.4b), in which they place both the index fingers and thumbs behind the ball to ensure a more secure catch. Goalkeepers of all ages should learn both these grips since they can be used at all levels of play.

Use the following points to teach your goalkeepers how to stop a shot at chest height:

- As the ball arrives, position your hands in the W-grip position or diamond as shown in figure 9.4, a and b.
- Extend your arms, slightly flexed at the elbows, toward the ball, and catch the ball with your fingertips (see figure 9.5a).
- Withdraw your arms to cushion the impact, and secure the ball to your chest (see figure 9.5b).

FIGURE 9.3 Stopping a ball at waist height.

FIGURE 9.4 *(a)* W-grip and *(b)* diamond grip.

FIGURE 9.5 Stopping a ball at chest height.

Lofted Shots

Shots that are at head height or higher are considered lofted shots. They are difficult for young goalkeepers to catch because doing so requires a greater ability to read the pace, spin, and trajectory of the ball than many young players have developed. Use the following points to teach your goalkeepers how to stop a shot that is lofted high into the air:

- Accurately judge the ball's path, and move toward the ball using a one-leg takeoff to generate maximum upward momentum; bend the front leg to increase the height of the jump (see figure 9.6a).

- Extend the arms overhead, and attempt to catch the ball at the highest point possible (see figure 9.6b).

- Secure the ball to the chest while landing (see figure 9.6c).

FIGURE 9.6 Stopping a ball that is lofted into the air.

Saving Shots

Saving shots requires good catching techniques. Sometimes the shot does not come directly at the goalkeeper, and he will have to move forward, backward, or laterally to make a save. A goalkeeper can save a shot by diving, collapsing, or jumping.

Diving

Sometimes your goalkeepers must dive to save a shot. Diving is necessary when an attacker strikes the ball hard and away from the goalkeeper and there is no time to step behind the flight of the ball with the entire body. Instead, the goalkeeper has to extend his body across the goalmouth to get his hands to the ball. Use the following points to teach your goalkeepers how to save shots:

- Step in the direction of the dive with the foot nearest the ball (e.g., step with the right foot to dive to the right), and push off that foot to begin the dive (see figure 9.7a).

- Extend the arms and hands toward the ball, and position the hands in a sideways W-grip (see figure 9.7b).

- Receive the ball on the fingertips and palms (see figure 9.7c).

- Place the lower hand behind the ball, tuck the elbows together to the front of the body, and pin the ball to the ground with your upper hand. Contact the ground with your side, not your belly (see figure 9.7d).

FIGURE 9.7   Diving to save a shot.

Some definitions will aid the coach and player in learning the skills of diving saves.

- *Low leg:* The one closest to the ground when in a horizontal position.
- *Low hand:* The one closest to the ground when in a horizontal position.
- *High leg:* The one farthest from the ground when in a horizontal position.
- *High hand:* The one farthest from the ground when in a horizontal position.
- *Takeoff leg:* The one on the side of the ball.
- *Trail leg:* The one opposite the side of the ball.
- *Near leg:* The one closest to the ball.
- *Far leg:* The one farthest from the ball.

COACHING TIP Teach diving saves to the U12 age group and up. This skill requires good timing, strength, and courage. Learning to dive is, for a goalkeeper, like learning to fly is for a pilot—the landing is the most important part. Teach players how to land first, how to take off next, and then how to fly across the goal.

Collapsing

Goalkeepers at times (typically for a low bouncing or rolling ball) have to collapse on a ball to secure it in tight quarters. As they secure the ball, they should collapse onto the side of the body, evenly distributing the force of impact and bringing the ball in and the top leg up in a fetal position (see figure 9.8). Instruct your keepers not to lie on their backs but to stay on their sides so they are always facing the field of play. This practice is especially important if they have fumbled the ball and need to pounce on it a second time. It also allows goalkeepers to immediately scan the field for where they want to distribute the ball.

FIGURE 9.8   Collapsing to save a shot.

Jumping

Goalkeepers may also come out of the goalmouth to jump to catch a high ball or deflect the ball over the crossbar (see figure 9.9). The ability to jump well gives the goalkeeper an even greater advantage in catching, punching, or deflecting a high ball. Add this jumping skill to fully extended arms above head height and the goalkeeper should dominate the air.

For more practice saving shots, see the activities on pages 156 and 157.

FIGURE 9.9   Jumping to save a shot.

Distributing the Ball

After a save, the keeper must distribute the ball to a teammate within 6 seconds by bowling, throwing, or kicking it. Each method is appropriate for different situations.

Bowling

Bowling the ball is a good choice for distributing the ball when a teammate's distance is 15 yards or less. The motion is similar to that used in regular bowling. Keepers should cup the ball in the palm of the hand, step toward their target with the opposite foot, and release with a bowling-type motion (see figure 9.10). They should release the ball smoothly at ground level so that it doesn't bounce.

FIGURE 9.10   Distributing the ball by bowling.

COACHING TIP   The decision about where to distribute the ball is tactical in nature; punting the ball downfield is not necessarily the best choice each time. Teach your players to always distribute to an open teammate, proceeding as for a field player's pass.

COACHING TIP   When bowling or throwing the ball, the goalkeeper's follow-through is crucial for maintaining accuracy. In both cases, teach your goalkeepers that the fingers of the throwing hand should follow through toward the target.

Throwing

For greater distance when distributing the ball, goalkeepers can throw the ball using an overhand motion similar to throwing a baseball, or they can use a three-quarter motion similar to throwing a javelin. Keepers should hold the ball in the palm of the hand, step toward the target, and use a baseball-style (see figure 9.11*a*) or three-quarter-style (see figure 9.11*b*) throwing motion.

FIGURE 9.11   Distributing the ball by throwing (*a*) baseball style and (*b*) three-quarter style.

Kicking

Although distributing the ball by using a kick is less accurate than throwing, it can send the ball quickly into the opponent's end of the field. The two most commonly used kicks are the full-volley punt and the drop kick.

Full-Volley Punt   Teach your goalkeepers the following points for the full-volley punt:

- Hold the ball in the palm of the hand, and extend the arm so that the ball is at or slightly below waist level (see figure 9.12*a*).

- Step forward with the nonkicking foot, release the ball, and contact the center of it with the instep, keeping shoulders and hips square to the target (see figure 9.12*b*).

- Kick through the point of contact, with the kicking foot going waist high (see figure 9.12*c*).

FIGURE 9.12   Distributing the ball using a volley kick.

Drop Kick The drop kick is another kick that goalkeepers can use when distributing the ball. It is similar to the full-volley punt except the keeper drops the ball (see figure 9.13a) and kicks it immediately after it touches the ground (see figure 9.13b). The flight of a drop-kicked ball is generally lower than that of a full volley punt (see figure 9.13c), making it a better choice on a blustery day or a quick counterattack opportunity.

For more practice distributing the ball, see the activities on pages 158 to 160.

FIGURE 9.13   Distributing the ball using a drop kick.

COACHING TIP   You may find that you have greater success teaching the drop kick to the U12 and U14 age groups because of the timing skills needed to kick the ball correctly and accurately.

Goalkeeping Set Play Techniques

When set plays occur in the defending third, the goalkeeper must take on a leadership role to organize the team. The keeper must give commands quickly, clearly, and confidently. Mental alertness and a strong physical presence are required of the keeper at such moments.

Corner Kick

The most crucial area for goalkeepers to defend consists of the goal area out to the penalty spot; it is commonly referred to as the danger zone. Instruct your goalkeeper to try to win any ball within the goal area (i.e., about 5 to 6 yards in front of the goal line) but not beyond unless there is a clear path to the ball.

Like the defending field players around her, the defending goalkeeper should also turn her hips a quarter turn outward to the field of play. In this way, she is not only in a better position to clear the ball upfield but also can see both the attack and the ball. For the goalkeeper, the technique of catching or punching the ball comes into play at corner kicks.

Free Kick (Direct or Indirect)

When defending against a free kick, the goalkeeper decides whether a wall needs to be set up and how many players should go into the wall. These decisions are based on the angle of the ball's path to the goal and the distance between the ball and the goal. As mentioned in chapter 8, the closer the ball is to the danger zone (see figure 8.6 on page 126), the more players will be needed in the wall.

Goal Kick

Once the goalkeeper has taken possession of the ball, he must attempt to use the opportunity in a way that an attack on the opposite goal can be set up. The keeper must give the goal kick the same tactical considerations as any other player: Where on the field should the ball be passed? Is a teammate open to receive the ball? Once the keeper answers such questions, the ball must be kicked so that it can be easily controlled over short distances or so that it gives teammates an advantage over long distances.

Penalty Kick

When defending against a penalty kick, only the goalkeeper is allowed inside the penalty area until the ball is kicked. The keeper must make thorough technical, tactical, and psychological preparations when handling a penalty kick. While a well-placed penalty kick is almost impossible to save, the keeper should know that by holding a central position in the goalmouth and refusing to be drawn in by fakes, he has a good chance of saving the shot should the kicker make even the slightest error. A goal is not a sure thing on a penalty kick. If nothing else, the goalkeeper may be able to block the ball to a defending player.

Throw-In

When a throw-in is taken by the opposing team in the goalkeeper's defending third, the keeper should analyze and then react to the situation similarly to how he would a corner kick. This is especially true if an opponent is capable of a long throw.

Goalkeeping Tactical Skills

The goalkeeper must be involved mentally in the tactics of the game at all times, so involve the goalkeeper in team training for tactics. The goalkeeper must be able to read the game as well as any other player on the team. In fact, goalkeepers often become the best tactically aware players on the team since they have the best view of the match.

Goalkeepers as Defenders

Clearly, goalkeeping is primarily a defensive role. Goalkeepers tend to grow in the position through three general stages. Those stages are shot blocker, shot stopper, and, finally, goalkeeper. The shot blocker stage is one where the goalkeeper simply reacts to shots after they have been taken. He tries to get into position to make saves, and this is sometimes merely blocking a shot and not making a clean catch. At the shot stopper stage, a player has progressed to not only making saves after a shot is taken but also being able to anticipate shots. The goalkeeper stage shows a player with all the talents of the shot stopper and then some. The goalkeeper is the complete package.

Goalkeepers as Attackers

The adage about goalkeepers being the last line of defense and the first line of attack may sound a bit trite, yet it remains a steadfast aspect of the game. Unfortunately, not enough thought has gone into the keeper's responsibilities on attack. Far too often the keeper who has just gained possession boots the ball upfield and then stations herself back in her goal, silently watching the match until the flow of play comes her way again. Furthermore, the kick is usually rushed, and no thought or attempt is made to place the ball in a certain location.

The keeper's responsibility on attack starts with her tactics on defense. The keeper must not be complacent and punch or deflect balls that she could catch. Obviously a much quicker, more precise counterattack can be started from the keeper's distribution.

Attacking Through Distribution

Once the keeper has possession, he must look upfield and go through a mental checklist of distribution options. With quickness of thought and speed of action, the keeper can turn defense into an attack. He should always look to the center of the field first and then to the flanks. If no teammates are available there, he should then look to the strikers, then the midfielders, and then the defenders. If the opportunity is available, distributing to the strikers or midfielders may start a quick counterattack. If possible, the keeper should place the ball into open space beyond the teammate it is being sent to so he may run onto the ball and toward the opposing team's goal.

If a buildup attack is called for, the goalkeeper should distribute to the midfielders or defenders. They then can take the attack upfield by interpassing. In all instances of distribution, the keeper should make a call to the player he passes to: "Turn," "Man on," "Pass back," and so on.

At times there may not be any good options for distribution for the counter-attack. When this is the case, the keeper should bowl the ball out to a defender and move to her to receive an immediate return pass. (This assumes that the keeper can play well with the ball at her feet.) During this time, players will be shifting positions, and an opening may occur for distribution.

There will also be times when the keeper will simply boot the ball upfield. This may be the case when no better distribution option is available and none can be created or if there is a great deal of pressure on the defense and they have been unsuccessful in playing the ball out of their own half. The entire team must move forward quickly in this instance, forcing the opponents to work to regain lost territory. This maneuver is also effective when there is a strong wind toward the opponents' half or when they must look up into the sun or rain for a high ball.

If the keeper is a good kicker, it is good strategy for him not to show his skill and power too soon in a match. It is better to give a few easy kicks early on and then later, when the opposing defense is well forward and perhaps square, loft a big kick into space behind them. With a long and accurate kick, the keeper can often bypass defenders and put his attackers in a straight race with opponents for the goal. This puts defenders at a disadvantage because they are facing their own goal and are under pressure from the forwards as well.

Attacking Outside the Penalty Area

After the keeper has distributed the ball and made her call, she should move up in her penalty area to become a supporting player to her teammates on and near the ball. The farther upfield the ball goes, the farther out the keeper should come. If the ball is well into her team's attacking third, there is absolutely no reason why the keeper should not advance beyond the penalty area. If a long ball is kicked into the keeper's half, she can go out and play it. This is the type of ball that might otherwise have simply been a footrace between the last defender and the first attacker.

Outside the penalty area, the keeper must play the ball as a field player would, so he should work on his field skills—clearance kicks, heading, and so on. Occasionally he should join in training games as a field player. Just as with his distributions, when the keeper comes out of the penalty area to play the ball, he should attempt to pass to a teammate or an advantageous space. Again, he must make a call after his pass. He should also talk constantly to teammates, giving instructions and encouragement.

If the keeper is outside the penalty area and the opposition gains possession, she immediately starts to retreat. She does this by running backward, not by turning away from the play to run forward—that is when a shot will be taken. The higher the level of play, the quicker the keeper must retreat, for players with strong kicks will be looking to catch the keeper too far out. If the ball is sent toward the goal but falls short, the keeper can always come forward to play it.

Cardinal Rules of Goalkeeping

Successful goalkeeping is largely about ingrained good habits that come second nature to the goalkeeper after years of training and game experience. Goalkeepers in the U10 to the U14 age groups discussed in this book will be in the initial phase of developing these habits. You should teach the following habits of top-class goalkeepers to the youngsters who will take on soccer's most demanding position.

1. Go for everything.

You may not be able to stop every shot that comes your way, but if you make the attempt, you will find that you are stopping shots you never before thought possible. You will also have the personal satisfaction that at least you made the attempt, and your teammates will be more forgiving even if you miss.

2. After a save, get up quickly.

If you have gone to the ground to make a save, get back on your feet as fast as possible. Look for a fast-break distribution or try to direct your teammates into position to receive a buildup distribution. This will particularly intimidate your opponents and raise the confidence of your teammates.

3. Don't be half-hearted—give 100 percent effort.

Every time you make a play, it must be with all of your ability. If you go halfway, you will miss saves and injure yourself.

4. Communicate loudly.

You must constantly give instructions when on defense. When your team is on the attack, come to the top of your penalty area or beyond, and talk to your teammates and offer support to the defenders. Be mentally involved in the entire match, no matter where the ball is.

5. No excuses! No whining! Just get on with the match.

If a goal is scored against you, a corner kick is given up, or the shot is a near miss, *do not* yell at your teammates, even if it was their fault. *Do not* hang your head or kick the ground or the post if it was your fault. During the match is no time to point fingers or make excuses. The play is over, so get on with playing the remainder of the match. Focus on what lies ahead!

Attacking in the Defending Third

Finally, on the team's dead-ball situations in the defending third, the keeper must become totally involved. His primary duty is goal kicks, which he should always take. This keeps the field players numerically balanced with the opposition. The keeper should attempt to pass to a teammate who is in a wide position and perhaps unmarked. On throw-ins and free kicks in the defending third, the keeper should make himself available to support.

The modern goalkeeper can be very effective in assisting her team's attack and defense and effectively inhibiting the attack of the opposition. When the keeper takes a more active role on attack, her concentration level will remain high, and her body will be looser and better prepared for her defensive responsibilities.

Goalkeeping Activities

The skills and concepts of good goalkeeping should be taught in gamelike activities, just like all the other skills in soccer when working with preadolescent players. The following activities engage young players in the fun of goalkeeping in a challenging and dynamic fashion. US Youth Soccer recommends that *all* children in the U10 to U14 age groups get exposed to playing goalkeeper. Begin this exposure to the position in training sessions and then matches.

➤ WHAT'S THE SCOOP?

Goal   To develop the ability to gather ground balls

Description   Play 2v1 in a playing area 20 yards long by 15 yards wide, with a goal set up at one end, as shown in the diagram. The 2 attackers try to score on the goalkeeper. The attackers take five shots on goal, passing between themselves and trying to get the best shot possible. The keeper is awarded 2 points for a clean scoop (one in which he cleanly gathers the ball) and 1 point for any other type of save. The goalkeeper receives

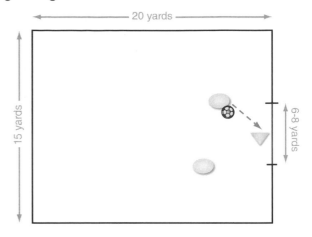

no points if a goal is scored. To restart play, the goalkeeper tosses the ball back to the attackers. After every five chances to defend the goal, rotate players so that everyone has a chance to play keeper.

- **U6 and U8:** This activity is not appropriate for these age groups.
- **U10:** Use a 6-yard-wide goal.
- **U12 and U14:** Use an 8-yard-wide goal.

Variations

- To make the activity easier for younger or less skilled players, increase the shot distance or decrease the speed of the shots.
- To make the activity more challenging for older or more skilled players, increase the speed of the shots or have players shoot to the corners.

➤ KEEPER WARS

Goal   To develop and encourage the basic diving technique for goalkeepers

Description   Play 1v1 in a playing area 20 yards long by 15 yard wide, with a 5-foot-high goal set up at one end, as shown in the diagram. One player positions in the goal and acts as a goalkeeper, and the other player shoots at the goal. To start, the goalkeeper gets five tries to dive and save using proper technique (this activity can also be adapted to focus on goalkeepers gathering air balls without diving for them). Award 1 point for each successful dive and save.

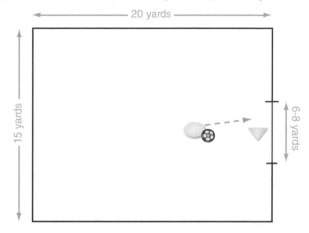

- **U6 and U8:** This activity is not appropriate for these age groups.
- **U10:** Use a 6-yard-wide goal; each player attempts to save 15 shots (15 is a perfect score).
- **U12 and U14:** Use an 8-yard-wide goal; each player attempts to save 20 shots (20 is a perfect score).

Variations

- To make the activity easier for younger or less skilled players, reduce the width of the goal or require shots from longer range.
- To make the activity more challenging for older or more skilled players, increase the width of the goal or add a player who tries to score goals from rebounds if the goalkeeper fails to deal with the shot effectively.

➤ BOWLING BALLS

Goal   To develop the ability to distribute the ball by bowling it

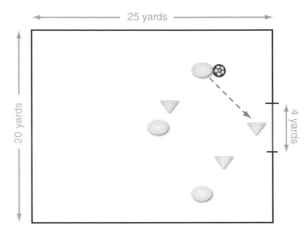

25 yards

20 yards

4 yards

Description   Play 3v3 in a playing area 25 yards long by 20 yards wide, with a 4-yard-wide goal set up at one end, as shown in the diagram. The 3 attacking players attack the goal as one defender drops back into the goal, making the game 3v2. When a shot is saved, either the goalkeeper or the player who made the save bowls the ball to a teammate. Award 1 point for each ball successfully bowled (one that is controlled by one of the keeper's teammates).

- **U6 and U8:** This activity is not appropriate for these age groups.
- **U10-U14:** Play 2v3 and utilize a goalkeeper as one of the offensive players, rotating goalkeepers after three attempts at bowling the ball.

Variations

- To make the activity easier for younger or less skilled players, play 1v3 or 2v4.
- To make the game more challenging for older or more skilled players, play 4v5.

➤ ON THE MONEY

Goal To develop the ability to distribute the ball by throwing it

Description Play 3v3 in a playing area 30 yards long by 20 yards wide, with a goal set up at one end, as shown in the diagram. The attacking team is awarded 1 point for each goal scored and for each distributed ball it gains possession of before the distributor's teammates. The defense is awarded 1 point each time a player successfully distributes the ball by throwing it to a teammate who can control the ball. Once the ball is distributed, begin play again, with the ball going back to the attack.

- **U6 and U8:** This activity is not appropriate for these age groups.
- **U10-U14:** Use an 8-yard-wide goal, and utilize a goalkeeper as one of the players on one of the teams; 10-minute playing time.

Variations

- To make the activity easier for younger or less skilled players, play 2v3 or 2v4.
- To make the activity more challenging for older or more skilled players, add a point for a distribution that is successfully received and controlled, beyond 15 yards for younger players and beyond 20 yards for older players.

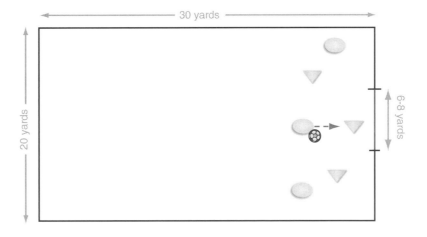

➤ PUNTING CONTEST

Goal To learn the proper technique for a goalkeeper punt

Description Play 1v1 in a field appropriate for the age group. Both players act as goalkeepers and begin the activity in the middle third of the field. One player has the ball to start and punts it toward the other player's goal line. This player tries to catch the ball as soon as possible. From the point on the field where she caught the ball, that player now punts back toward the other player's goal line. The objective is to be the first to force the other player over her goal line.

- **U6 and U8:** This activity is not appropriate for these age groups.
- **U10:** Play on a 60-by-45-yard field.
- **U12:** Play on an 80-by-55-yard field.
- **U14:** Play on a 105-by-65-yard field.

Variation Award a bonus point to the keeper each time he can catch the punt at the highest point possible.

Matches provide opportunities for your players to show what they've

learned in training and practice. Just as your players' focus shifts on match days from learning and training to competing, your focus shifts from teaching skills to coaching players as they perform those skills in matches. Of course, the match is a teaching opportunity as well, but the focus is on performing what has been learned, participating, and having fun.

In previous chapters you learned how to teach your players techniques and tactics; in this chapter you will learn how to coach your players as they execute those techniques and tactics in matches. We provide important coaching principles that will guide you before, during, and after a match.

Before the Match

Many coaches focus on how they will coach only during the actual match; instead, preparations should begin well before the kickoff of the match. A day or two before a match, you should cover several subjects—in addition to techniques and tactics—to prepare your players for the match. Depending on the age group you are working with, create a specific game plan for the opponent based on information that is available to you; make decisions on specific team tactics you want to use; and discuss pregame particulars such as what to eat before the match, what to wear, and when to be at the field.

Deciding Team Tactics

Some coaches burn the midnight oil as they devise a complex plan of attack for matches. Team tactics at the youth level, however, don't need to be complex—especially for the younger age groups. The main focus should be the importance of teamwork, the responsibility of every player to fulfill their roles, and the importance of every player to try their best and work to help teammates. The older the age group and the more familiar you become with your team's capabilities, the more you can then help them focus on specific tactics.

During the week before a match, coaches of U12 and U14 players should inform them of the tactics they plan to use against the particular opponent. Regardless of the tactical adjustments you might make for a particular opponent, remember it is far more important that you teach players the proper execution of individual, group, and team tactics and focus their attention on bringing the skills they have learned in training to the match.

> **COACHING TIP** Based on the age level, experience, and knowledge of your players, you may want to let them help you determine the team formation for the match. Allowing player input helps your players learn the game, involves them at a planning level often reserved solely for the coach, and gives them a feeling of ownership. Rather than just carrying out the coach's orders, they're executing the game plan they helped create.

Creating a Game Plan

Just as you need a practice plan for what you will cover at each training session, you also need a game plan for match day. As a coach, your game plan for youth soccer will vary depending on the age group with which you are working. As you begin planning and mapping out how your match days will progress, keep the following age-related points in mind.

U6 and U8	• Encourage players to try their best. • Relax and let them, and yourself, enjoy the spirit of the game.
U10	• Focus on helping your team execute what they have learned. The strengths and weaknesses of the opposition are of little concern at this age. • Give players simple team formations that make it easy to support each other and execute the techniques and tactics learned in practice. • Remind players to focus on one offensive and one defensive aspect that they have learned for the game.
U12 and U14	• Help players focus on one or two of the opposition's strengths and weaknesses. • Introduce (as possible) adjustments to play based on the opponent, but continue to give priority to properly executing the techniques and tactics learned in practice. • Introduce more complex team formations that now include a midfield line.

Discussing Pregame Preparations

Players need to know what to do before a match, such as what and when they should eat on game day, what clothing to wear to the match, what equipment to bring, what time to arrive at the field, and how the warm-up will run. Discuss these particulars with them at the last practice before a match. Here are guidelines for discussing these issues.

Pregame Meal

The general goals of the pregame meal are to fuel the players for the upcoming event, maximize carbohydrate stores, and provide energy to the brain. Some foods, such as those containing carbohydrate and protein, digest more quickly than others; we suggest that players consume these foods rather than fat, which digests more slowly. Good carbohydrate foods include spaghetti, rice, and bran. Good protein foods include low-fat yogurt and skinless chicken. Players should eat foods they are familiar with and that they can digest easily. Big meals should be eaten three to four hours before the match. Players who don't have time for a big meal can consume sport beverages and replacement meals.

Many soccer matches are played early in the morning at the youth level, particularly for the U6 and U8 age groups, so a light breakfast an hour or two before the game is best. However, you do not need to waken a six-year-old to eat a pregame meal at 6 a.m. for an 8 a.m. kickoff. A light snack before the game is acceptable in these situations.

Clothing and Equipment

Instruct players to wear their uniforms to the field. They should put on soccer shin guards, socks, and shoes once they arrive at the field. You should also teach children to take off their soccer shoes and shin guards immediately after the match. This habit extends the life of the equipment and gives the lower legs and feet a chance to recover through improved circulation.

Youth players from the U6 to U14 age groups should typically wear molded or turf shoes. All cleats, studs, or bars on shoes may not be less than one-half inch wide and not longer than three-fourths of an inch. Aluminum, leather, rubber, nylon, and plastic cleats are legal. Screw-in studs, however, should be used only by adolescent and older players (U15 to U19) and should not be used at the younger levels.

Players may not wear equipment with projecting metal or other hard plates or with exposed sharp edges, such as metal knee braces or hard casts. They also may not wear pads containing hard or unyielding materials, even those covered with soft padding.

Arrival Time

Your players need to adequately warm up before a match, so instruct them to arrive early enough before game time to go through the team warm-up (which you will read about in a later section), and tell them where to gather on the field. The appropriate amount of time depends on the age group of the team. Following are suggested times for youth age groups.

- *U6 and U8:* 10 minutes before kickoff
- *U10:* 15 minutes before kickoff
- *U12:* 20 minutes before kickoff
- *U14:* 25 minutes before kickoff

Also, consider making a team rule stating that players must show up a pre-designated amount of time before a match and go through the complete team warm-up or they won't start. This rule teaches accountability and punctuality to youngsters. Additionally, it gets players into good habits for getting their bodies and minds ready for match play.

Warm-Up

Players need to prepare both physically and mentally for a match once they arrive at the field, and physical preparation involves warming up. We've suggested that players arrive 10 to 25 minutes before the match to warm up, depending on the age group. Make the match warm-up similar to training warm-ups. The warm-up should consist of a few brief games or activities that focus on skill practice, stretches, and range-of-motion exercises. Before match day, it is also a good idea to walk through the steps for how the team will take the field and where on the field the players will warm up. Following are suggested warm-up activities for youth age groups.

- *U6:* Players warm up with the ball individually by practicing skills such as dribbling and juggling.
- *U8:* Players begin with an individual warm-up and then move into pairs and do simple passing and receiving activities.
- *U10-U14:* Players begin with an individual warm-up and then move into group activities such as a small-sided game (5v5); include a warm-up for goalkeepers that focuses on their skills. U14 players may also want to practice their part in set plays.

> **COACHING TIP** Although the site coordinator and officials have formal responsibilities for facilities and equipment, you should know what to look for to ensure that the match is safe for all players (see Facilities and Equipment Checklist on page 190). You should arrive at the field 5 to 10 minutes earlier than you asked the players to arrive so that you can check the field, check in with the site coordinator and officials, and greet your players as they arrive to warm up.

Refrain from delivering a long-winded pep talk, but you can help players mentally prepare for the match by reminding them of the skills they've been working on in recent training sessions and focusing their attention on what they've been doing well. Take time to remind players that they should work as a team, play hard and smart, and have fun.

Unplanned Events

Part of being prepared to coach is to expect the unexpected. What do you do if players are late? What if *you* have an emergency and can't make the match or will be late? What if the match is rained out or otherwise postponed? Being prepared to handle out-of-the-ordinary circumstances will help you if and when unplanned events happen.

If players are late, you may have to adjust your starting lineup. Although this may not be a major inconvenience, stress to your players that there are important reasons for being on time. First, part of being a member of a team is being committed to and responsible for the other members. When players don't show up or

Communicating With Parents

The groundwork for your communication with parents will have been laid in the parent orientation meeting, through which parents learned the best ways to support the efforts of their kids (and the whole team) on the field. Help parents judge success based not just on the outcome of the match but also on how the kids are improving their performances.

If parents yell at the kids for their mistakes during the match, make disparaging remarks about the referees or opponents, or shout instructions for which tactics to use, ask them to stop and to instead support the team through their comments and actions. These standards of conduct should be covered in the preseason parent orientation.

When time permits, as parents gather at the field before a match and before the team takes the field, you can let them know in a general sense what the team has been focusing on during the past week and what your goals are for the match. The parents can be a great asset to the coaches and the team by applauding the efforts of the kids on the field. Their support is especially helpful when the coach has prepped them on what to cheer for in relation to the new techniques and tactics the players are learning. Your players must come first during this time, however, so focus on the kids during the pregame warm-up.

After a match, quickly come together as a staff and decide what to say to the team. Then informally assess with parents, as the opportunity arises, how the team did based not on the outcome but on meeting performance goals and playing to the best of their ability. Help parents see the contest as a process, not solely as a test that is pass–fail or win–lose. Encourage parents to reinforce that concept at home. For more information on communicating with parents, see page 16 of chapter 2.

show up late, they break that commitment. Second, players need to warm up to physically and mentally prepare for the match. Skipping the warm-up risks injury.

A time may come when an emergency causes you to be late or miss a match. In these cases, notify your assistant coach (if you have one), your team manager, or the league coordinator. If notified in advance, another volunteer or a parent of a player might be able to step in for the match.

Sometimes a match must be postponed because of inclement weather or for reasons such as unsafe field conditions. If the postponement takes place before game day, call every member of your team to let them know. If it happens while the teams are on the field preparing for the match, gather your team members and explain why the match has been postponed. Make sure all your players have a ride home before you leave—you should be the last to go.

During the Match

Throughout the match, you must keep the competition in proper perspective and help your players do the same. Observe how your players execute techniques and tactics and how well they play together. These observations can help you decide appropriate practice plans for the following week. Let's take a more detailed look at your responsibilities during a match.

Tactical Decisions

Although you may not be called on to create a complex match strategy, as mentioned earlier, you are called on to make tactical decisions throughout a match. You must make decisions about who starts the match, when to enter substitutes, whether to make slight adjustments to your team's tactics, and how to deal with players' performance errors.

Starting and Substituting Players

When considering playing time, make sure everyone on the team gets to play at least half of each match. This principle should guide you as you consider starting and substitution patterns. We suggest you consider two options in substituting players:

1. **Substitute individually.**

Replace one player with another. This method offers you a lot of latitude in deciding who goes in when, and it gives you the most combinations of players throughout the match. Another advantage is that it does not disrupt the playing rhythm of the team. It can be hard to keep track of each child's playing time, but assigning an assistant or a parent to this task can make it easier. Be aware that national rules require a 50 percent playing time for all players.

Keeping a Proper Perspective

Winning matches is the short-term goal of your soccer program. The long-term goals are equally important: learning the techniques, tactics, and rules of soccer; becoming fit; and becoming good sports in soccer and in life. Your young players are winning when they are becoming better people through their participation in soccer. You have the privilege of setting the tone for how your team approaches the match. Keep winning and all aspects of the competition in proper perspective, and your young charges will most likely follow suit.

2. **Substitute after quarters or at halftime.**

The advantages of substituting players after each quarter (especially at the U6 and U8 levels) are that you can easily track playing time and players know how long they will be in before they might be replaced. Some coaches choose to make substitutions only at halftime.

Adjusting Team Tactics

As mentioned earlier in this chapter, you will make few, if any, tactical adjustments during a match. It is far more important for your players to focus on properly executing the tactics you have taught them during training than on making adjustments during the match. For the U6, U8, and U10 age groups, do not plan on making any tactical adjustments during the match. For the U12 and U14 age groups, make only minor adjustments that fall within the scope of what the players have already learned. You may want to consider the following questions when adjusting team tactics:

- How do the opposing players usually initiate their attacks? Do they aim to get around, over, or through your defense? Identifying their strategy can help you make defensive adjustments.

- Who are the strongest and weakest players on the opposing team? As you identify strong players, you'll want to assign your more skilled defending players to mark them.

- Are the opponent's forwards fast and powerful? Do they come to the ball, or do they try to run behind the defense and receive passes? Their mode of attack should influence how you instruct your players to mark them.

- On defense, do the opposing players play a high-pressure game, or do they retreat once you've gained possession of the ball? Each type of defense could call for a different strategy.

Determining the answers to such questions can help you formulate an effective game plan and make proper adjustments as the match progresses. However, don't stress tactics too much during a match. Doing so can take the fun out of the game for the players. If you don't trust your memory, carry a pen and pad to note which team tactics and individual skills need attention at the next training session.

Correcting Players' Errors

In chapter 6 you learned about two types of errors: learning errors and performance errors. Learning errors are those that occur because players don't know how to perform a skill. Performance errors are made not because players don't know how to execute the skill but because they make mistakes in carrying out what they do know.

Sometimes it's not easy to tell which type of error players are making. Knowing your players' capabilities helps you determine whether they know the skill and are simply making mistakes in executing it or whether they don't know how to perform it. If they are making learning errors, note the problem and cover it at the next training session. Match time is not the time to teach skills.

If they are making performance errors, however, you can help players correct them during a match. Players who make performance errors often do so because they have a lapse in concentration or motivation (or they are simply demonstrating human error). Competition and contact can also adversely affect a young player's technique, and a word of encouragement about concentration may help. If you do correct a performance error during a match, do so in a quiet, controlled, and positive tone of voice, either during a break or when the player is on the touchline with you.

> **COACHING TIP** Designate an area on the touchline where players gather after coming off the field. In this area, you can speak to them either individually or as a group and make necessary adjustments.

For those making performance errors, you must determine whether the error is just an occasional error that anyone can make or whether it is an expected error for a youngster at that stage of development. If the latter is the case, then the player may appreciate your not commenting; she knows it was a mistake and may already know how to correct it. On the other hand, perhaps an encouraging word and a coaching cue ("Remember to follow through on your shots!") are just what the player needs. Knowing the players and judging what to say is an essential part of the art of coaching.

Coach and Player Behavior

Another aspect of coaching on game day is managing behavior—both your players' and your own. Being composed and focused during the match is crucial for good performance on the part of both players and coaches.

Coach Conduct

You greatly influence your players' behavior before, during, and after a match. If you're up, your players are more likely to be up. If you're anxious, they'll take notice and the anxiety can become contagious. If you're negative, they'll respond with worry. If you're positive, they'll play with more enjoyment. If you're constantly yelling instructions or commenting on mistakes, it will be difficult for players to concentrate.

Focus instead on positive competition and on having a good time. Let players get into the flow of the match. A coach who overorganizes everything and dominates a match from the touchline is definitely not making the game fun. So how should you conduct yourself on the touchline? Here are a few pointers:

- Be calm, in control, and supportive of your players.
- Encourage players often during play, but instruct sparingly. Players should focus on their performance, not on directions shouted from the team bench.

- If you need to instruct a player, do so when you're both on the touchline, in an unobtrusive manner. Never yell at players for making a mistake. Instead, briefly demonstrate or remind them of the correct technique and then encourage them. Tell them how to correct the problem on the field.

You should also make certain that you have discussed touchline demeanor as a staff and that everyone is in agreement about the way they will conduct themselves—then stick with it. Remember, you're not playing for the World Cup. In this program, soccer competitions are designed to help players develop their skills and character and have fun. Coach during matches in a manner that helps your players achieve these goals.

Player Conduct

It is the responsibility of coaches and parents to teach good sporting behavior and to keep players under control, from the U6 age group on up. Do so by setting a good example and disciplining when necessary. Set team rules for good behavior. If players attempt to cheat, fight, argue, badger, yell disparaging remarks, and so forth, it is your responsibility to correct the misbehavior. Initially it may mean removing players immediately from the match, letting them calm down, and then speaking to them quietly. Explain that their behavior is not acceptable for your team and that if they want to play, they must not repeat the action.

COACHING TIP Overly competitive trends are not only adversely affecting the essence of player development but also blurring the line between ethical and unethical behavior. It is our mission to use soccer as the vehicle to "develop character, instill values, teach respect for authority and society, develop confidence and a positive self-image, and help youth reach their potential in life" (US Youth Soccer Player Development Model, 2011).

Consider team rules in these areas of match conduct:

- Player language
- Player behavior
- Interactions with officials
- Discipline for misbehavior
- Dress code for matches

Player Welfare

All players are not the same. Some attach their self-worth to winning and losing. This idea is fueled by coaches, parents, peers, and others in society who place great emphasis on winning. Players become anxious when they're uncertain whether they can meet the expectations of others—especially when meeting a particular expectation is important to them also.

If your players look uptight and anxious during a match, find ways to ease their worries about their performance and to reduce the importance they are attaching to the match. Help players focus on realistic personal goals that are attainable and measurable and that will help them improve their performance while they have fun. Another way to reduce anxiety on game day is to stay away from emotional pregame pep talks. Instead, remind players of the techniques and tactics they will use, and encourage them to play hard, do their best, and have fun.

When coaching during matches, remember that the most important outcome from playing soccer is each player's increased self-worth. Keep that objective firmly in mind, and strive to promote it through every coaching decision.

Opponents and Referees

Respect opponents and referees because without them, there wouldn't be a match. Opponents provide opportunities for your team to test itself, improve, and excel. Referees help provide a fair and safe experience for players and, as appropriate, help them learn the game.

You and your team should show respect for opponents and referees by being polite and putting forth your best efforts. Don't allow your players to trash-talk or taunt an opponent or a referee. Such behavior is disrespectful to the spirit of the competition, and you should immediately remove a player from a match, as discussed previously, if he disobeys your team rules in this area.

Remember, too, that referees at this level are quite often teenagers—in many cases not much older than the players themselves—and the level of officiating should be commensurate with the level of play. In other words, don't expect perfection from referees any more than you do from your own players. They won't make every call, especially at younger levels, because to do so would stop the match every 10 seconds. You may find that referees at younger levels call only the most flagrant penalties, those directly affecting the outcome of the match. As long as they are making calls consistently on both sides and addressing the penalties, most of your officiating concerns will be met.

Keeping the Match Safe

Chapter 4 is devoted to player safety, but it's worth noting here that safety during matches can be affected by how referees call the game. If referees don't call rules correctly and thus risk injury to your players, you must intervene. Voice your concern in a respectful manner that places the emphasis where it should be: on the players' safety. One of the referee's main responsibilities is to look after everyone's safety, and the referee should work with coaches to protect the players as much as possible. Don't hesitate to address a safety issue with a referee when the need arises.

After the Match

When the match is over, join your team in congratulating the coaches and players of the opposing team, and then be sure to thank the referees. Bring players together to cool down briefly and to replenish fluids. Check on any injuries, and inform players how to care for them. Be prepared to speak with the referees about problems that occurred during the match. Then hold a brief meeting (which we discuss later) to ensure your players are on an even keel, whether they won or lost.

Reactions After a Match

Your first concern after a match should be your players' attitudes and mental well-being. You don't want them to be too high after a win or too low after a loss. After the match is when you can most influence them to keep the outcome in perspective and settle their feelings.

When celebrating a victory, make sure your team does so in a way that doesn't show disrespect for the opponents. It's appropriate to be happy about a win, but don't allow your players to taunt the opponents or boast about their victory. If they've lost, your team will naturally be disappointed. But if they've made a winning effort, let them know it. Help them be proud and maintain a positive attitude that will carry over to the next training session and match. Winning and losing are a part of life, not just a part of sport. If players learn to handle both well, they'll have a skill they can apply to whatever they do.

> **COACHING TIP**   The total time from the start of the cool-down to the conclusion of the postgame meeting should be approximately 2 minutes for the U6 age group, increasing with older groups to a maximum of 10 minutes for the U14 group.

Postgame Team Meeting

After the match, gather your team in a designated area for a short meeting. Before this meeting, decide as a staff what to say and who will say it. Be sure the staff members speak with one voice after the match.

If your players have performed well, compliment and congratulate them. Whether they've won or lost, tell them specifically what they did with proficiency. Such commendation will reinforce their desire to repeat their good performances. Don't use this time to criticize individual performances or thrash out tactical problems, either. You should help players improve their skills, but do so at the next training session—they won't absorb much tactical information immediately after the match.

Finally, make sure your players have transportation home. Be the last one to leave to ensure full supervision of your players.

Developing Season and Training Plans

11

PLANS

We hope you've learned a lot from this book: what your responsibilities are as a coach, how to communicate well and provide for safety, how to teach and shape skills, and how to coach on match days. But match days make up only a portion of your season—you and your players will spend more time in training than in matches. How well you conduct training sessions and prepare your players for competition will greatly affect not only your players' enjoyment and success throughout the season but also your own.

Season Plans

Your season plan acts as a snapshot of the entire season. Before the first training session with your players, you must sit down as a staff and develop one. To do so, simply write down each training and match date on a calendar, and then go back and number the training sessions. These training numbers are the foundation of your season plan. Now you can work through the plan, moving from session to session, and outline what you hope to cover in each training session

Fun Learning Environment

Regardless of what point you're at in your season, work to create an environment that welcomes learning and promotes teamwork. Following are seven tips to help you and your staff get the most out of your training sessions:

1. Stick to the training times agreed on as a staff.
2. Start and end each training session as a team.
3. Keep the training routine as consistent as possible so that the players can feel comfortable.
4. Be organized in your approach by moving quickly from one activity to another and from one stage of training to another.
5. Tell your players what training will include before the training session starts.
6. Allow the players to take water breaks whenever possible.
7. Focus on providing positive feedback.

In addition to trying the activities provided throughout chapters 7, 8, and 9 in this book, you may also want to consider using gamelike activities to add variety and make training more fun. Doing gamelike activities during each training session prepares players for many different situations that arise in matches. You will find gamelike activities on page 55 at the end of chapter 5.

by noting the purpose of the training, the main skills you will cover, and the activities you will use. Keep in mind that having too many matches in a player's schedule becomes a hindrance to development. You must strike the right balance among the number of matches per season, the number of training sessions per season, and the amount of time off. Planned time off is vitally important to prevent overuse injuries and mental burnout. Both players and coaches need time off to recharge their batteries and come back reinvigorated.

> **COACHING TIP** While developing your season plan, keep in mind that you will want to incorporate the games approach into your training sessions. The games approach is superior to the traditional approach since it focuses on replicating the game environment. Using gamelike activities better prepares the players, both physically and mentally, for the demands of the game.

Following is more detailed information about season plans for each age group: U6, U8, U10, U12, and U14.

U6 Season Plan

The players in this age group will be new to playing soccer. The ball-to-player ratio at this age should be 1:1, so you must plan for individual activities in your training sessions. For the U6 age group, plan to cover the following concepts and skills during the soccer season:

- *Psychology:* Sharing, fair play, parental involvement, how to play (e.g., getting along with others), and emotional management
- *Fitness:* Balancing, running, jumping, introduction to warming up, and movement education
- *Techniques:* Dribbling and shooting
- *Tactics:* Where the field is, field boundaries, and which goal to kick at

U8 Season Plan

Some of the players in this age group will have been exposed to soccer, but others will be new to the sport. The ball-to-player ratios at this age should be 1:1 and 1:2, so prepare for both individual and paired activities during training sessions. For the U8 age group, plan to cover these concepts and skills during the soccer season:

- *Psychology:* Working in pairs, fair play, parental involvement, how to play (e.g., getting along with others), and emotional management
- *Fitness:* Agility, eye–foot and eye–hand coordination, introduction to cooling down, and movement education

- *Techniques:* Ball lifting and juggling, block tackles, receiving ground balls with the inside and sole of the foot, shooting with the inside of the foot, toe passes and shots, throw-ins, and introduction to the push pass
- *Tactics:* Introduction to all positions and their names, and 1v1 attack

U10 Season Plan

Many of these kids will have played soccer, but some may still be novices. The ball-to-player ratio should be 1:3, so you can plan for individual, paired, and small group activities. For the U10 age group, you should cover the following concepts and skills during the soccer season:

- *Psychology:* Working in small groups, focusing for one entire half, sensitivity, how to win and lose gracefully, fair play, parental involvement, how to play (e.g., getting along with others), communication, and emotional management
- *Fitness:* Endurance, range of motion, flexibility, and proper warm-up and cool-down (now mandatory)
- *Techniques:* Running with the ball, passing, instep drives, receiving ground balls with the instep and outside of the foot, receiving bouncing balls with the instep (cushioning) and with the sole or inside or outside of the foot (wedging), dribbling fakes, and introduction to heading and crossing; for goalkeepers—ready stance, diamond grip, holding the ball after a save, W-grip, catching, shots at the keeper, punting, and introduction to goal kicks and throwing
- *Tactics:* 1v1 defending, roles of first attacker and defender, 2v1 attacking, man-to-man defense, and introduction to set plays

U12 Season Plan

Most of the players in this age group will have had exposure to soccer, but some may be newer to the sport. The season plan for this age group builds on the U6 to U10 season plans as players practice and refine fundamental skills. The ball-to-player ratio is 1:5, so you can plan for individual, paired, small group, and larger group activities. For the U12 age group, cover the following concepts and skills during the soccer season:

- *Psychology:* Teamwork, confidence, desire, mental rehearsal, intrinsic motivation, handling distress, how to learn from each match, fair play, parental involvement, how to play (e.g., getting along with others), and emotional management
- *Fitness:* Speed, strength, and aerobic exercise
- *Techniques:* Feints with the ball, receiving balls (rolling, bouncing, and in the air) with various parts of the body (foot, thigh, chest, and head), heading (both standing and jumping) to score goals and clear the ball,

chipping to score, passing with the outside of the foot, bending shots, crossing to near-post and penalty spot spaces, heel passes, kicking and receiving with the inside of the instep, introduction to half-volley and volley shooting, and introduction to slide tackle; for goalkeepers—footwork, bowling, low diving and forward diving, angle play, near-post play, saving penalty kicks, and introduction to parrying and boxing

- *Tactics:* 2v1 defending, 2v2 attacking and defending, roles of second attacker and defender, combination passing, verbal and visual communication for all positions, commanding the goalmouth for the goalkeeper, halftime analysis, corner kick plays (defending and attacking), kickoff play, wall pass, identifying potential roles for players (goalkeeper, defender, midfielder, or forward), and reinforcing the principles of attack

U14 Season Plan

Most of the players in this age group have some experience with soccer, but a few may be newer to the sport. The season plan for this age group builds on the U6 to U12 season plans as players further refine the skills they have learned from past years. The season plan for this age group also introduces several new skills, including heading, diving, and collapsing for goalkeepers. The ball-to-player ratio for this age group is 1:8, so you can plan for individual, paired, and both small and large group activities. For the U14 age group, cover the following concepts and skills during the soccer season:

- *Psychology:* Assertiveness, tension control, self-discipline and team discipline, staying focused for an entire match, fair play, parental involvement, how to play (e.g., getting along with others), mental focusing techniques, and emotional management

- *Fitness:* Power, acceleration, anaerobic exercise, and cardiorespiratory and cardiovascular training

- *Techniques:* Chipping to pass, bending passes, crossing to far-post area and top of the penalty area, half-volley and volley shooting, slide tackles, heading to pass, flick headers, diving headers, kicking and receiving with the outside of the instep, outside-of-foot shot, dummying the ball, shoulder charge; for goalkeepers—far-post play, medium and high diving, parrying over the crossbar and around the posts, boxing and catching crosses, half volley (drop kick), kick saves, and long overarm throws

- *Tactics:* Individual and group tactics, compactness, commanding the goal area for the goalkeeper, role of third defender, making recovery and tracking runs, throw-ins, penalty kick and free-kick plays (defending and attacking), defending the defensive third playing in the attacking third, postgame analysis, checking runs, takeovers, switching positions during the flow of play, providing attacking support out to the penalty spot for the goalkeeper, zone defense, and reinforcing the principles of defense

Training Plans

Coaches rarely believe they have enough time to practice everything they want to cover. Training plans help you organize your thoughts so that you stay on track with your training objectives. They also help you better visualize and prepare so that you can run your training sessions effectively.

First, your training plans should be age appropriate for the group you are coaching, incorporating all the skills and concepts you wrote into the season plan for that age group. The core of your training plan should include activities that move from simple to more complex and that focus on the skills highlighted in the season plan. The plan for each training session should note the training objective and the equipment necessary to execute specific activities. It should also include a warm-up and a cool-down.

Remember that during the cool-down, coaches should attend to any injuries incurred during training and make sure that players drink plenty of water. It is also a good idea to have them loosen shoelaces to help circulation in the feet and, beginning with the U10 age group, loosen or take off their shin guards to aid blood flow to the lower legs. Such provisions for player well-being should be part of every training session.

Sample U6 Training Plan

Objective
Dribbling

Equipment
1 ball for each player, 2 small goals (cones or bicycle flags can be used in lieu of goals), 12 cones, 10 training bibs (5 of one color and 5 of another)

Activity	Description	Coaching points
Warm-up (5 min)	Practice balance activities such as standing on one foot, one- and two-leg hopping, and skipping.	• Balance • Agility • Coordination
Free-form dribbling (10 min)	Every player needs a ball. Start by having players dribble around each other in a 10 × 10 yd area. The space can be marked off with cones. Next, have all players toss up a ball and then dribble the first ball found. Vary the pace at which the players dribble around each other (fast, slow-motion, and medium speeds).	• Body and mind preparation • Eye–hand coordination and general movement abilities • Ball control and balance

Activity	Description	Coaching points
Shadow dribbling (5 min)	Mark off a 20 × 20 yd grid. Each player dribbles a ball and follows the coach, who is also dribbling a ball. Coach executes basic dribbling moves and silly movements for players to mimic. Include dribbling basics and tumbling, balancing, and rhythmic exercises.	• Dribbling and movement enhancement • Decision making • Enjoyment
Knee tag (5 min)	Players position with a ball in a 10 × 15 yd area. Players dribble their balls and try to tag others on the knee. Each player gets 1 point for a tag.	• Physical fitness components • Dribbling and shielding skills • Looking around (vision)
3v3 match (15 min)	Play a 3v3 match according to US Youth Soccer modification rules for the U6 age group. Use two goals, one ball, and no goalkeepers. Use cones to mark out a 25 × 15 yd playing area with small goals. The smaller space allows for end-to-end action with shots on the goal. Have one extra team of equal numbers. Rotate in the third team after a goal is scored or every 3 min, whichever comes first. This allows for recovery.	• Summation of all challenges for the players (remember—stay out of their way and let them play)
Cool-down (5 min)	Body shapes: Players create as many different shapes as they can with their bodies. Coach prompts change of movement.	• Lowering heart rate and body temperature • Body control • Creativity and fun

US Youth Soccer

Sample U8 Training Plan

Objective
Teamwork

Equipment
1 ball for each player, 2 small goals (cones or bicycle flags can be used in lieu of goals), 24 cones, 12 training bibs (6 of one color and 6 of another)

Activity	Description	Coaching points
Warm-up (5 min)	Soccer marbles: Players divide into pairs; each player has a ball on the ground. Player A passes his ball and tries to hit player B's ball. After both balls stop rolling, player B makes a pass to try to hit player A's ball, and so on. Each ball must be stationary before a pass is made. Players may not block the path of the pass.	• Gradual warm-up of the muscles without overexertion • Repeated practice of passing accuracy • Competition and fun
Juggling with a partner (10 min, played in 3 min increments)	Two players compete against each other in pairs to keep the ball up in the air using as many touches as needed in a 3 min period. Rest for 10 sec between bouts to emphasize coaching points.	• Movement behind and in line with the ball • Early surface selection
Soccer Newcomb (10 min)	Mark off a 20 × 15 yd grid, with 1 yd of dead space for the net. Using a size 3 ball that is not too inflated, two teams of 2 play toss–receive–catch over the net. If the ball is caught, the team that catches it receives 1 point; if the ball hits the ground, the team receives no points and must toss the ball to the other side. The opposing team then has a chance to catch the ball.	• Movement behind and in line with the ball • Early surface selection • Withdrawing on contact
Volley game (5 min, played in 30 sec increments)	Set up 15 × 15 yd grids, with two players and one ball per grid. The players freely pass a ball inside the grid, trying to keep the ball in the air. The ball may not bounce more than twice before it is played. Count the number of passes inside the grid. Each pass is 1 point; players try to get more points than other pairs in 30 sec.	• Getting in line of flight quickly • Being ready and balanced to receive • Choosing body surface • Withdrawing surface • Scooping or spooning ball with foot

Activity	Description	Coaching points
Pong (10 min)	Sharing a ball, two players play against each other. They place two cones anywhere from 2 to 8 yd apart. Let them choose. The players then pass back and forth to each other. The ball must never stop, must always stay on the ground, and must go through the two cones without touching them. Whenever a rule is violated, the other player receives 1 point. Because the ball must never stop, players have to play 1-2 touch. The closer the two cones are, the closer the pairs are probably going to be; the farther apart they are, the more they will have to move laterally (much like the old arcade game of the same name). Play for a set time, and see who can become the Pong champ!	• Staying balanced • Being quick on the feet • Movement behind the ball • Striking through the center of the ball • Following through with the kicking foot toward the target
2v2 get outta there! (15 min)	The players are in two teams. The coach controls the balls. He passes one ball onto the field to start play. Two players from each team play until a goal is scored or the ball goes out of bounds. If the ball goes out of bounds, the coach yells, "Get outta there!" and two new players from each team come on the field with the next ball. Once a goal is scored, the two players who scored stay on, and two new players from the other team come on the field to play against them.	• See through the bottom of the eyes • Keep ball rolling • First try to solve game by dribbling • Player without ball finds big, easy spot to receive a pass
Cool-down (5 min)	The long and the short of it: Players sit on the ground, and the coach asks them to show how small they can make their bodies, how long, how wide, what shape, and so forth.	• Lowering heart rate and body temperature • Body control • Creativity, imagination, and fun

US Youth Soccer

PLANS

Sample U10 Training Plan

Objective
Use of space

Equipment
1 ball for each player, 2 regulation goals for the U10 age group (cones or corner flags can be used in lieu of goals), 24 cones, 4 corner flags, 22 training bibs (11 of one color and 11 of another)

Activity	Description	Coaching points
Warm-up (10 min)	Ball master: Divide players into groups of four. Every group gives their ball to the coach, or ball master, who tosses the ball out for each group to collect individually. Players bring the ball back: 1. With three elbows and one knee, picking up the ball and running back to the coach. 2. With feet, using 7 touches to return it to the ball master. 3. With feet, using 17 touches to return it to the ball master. 4. With feet, using 2 touches to return it to the ball master. The coach walks around while the groups bring the ball back to her.	• Increasing circulation and loosening joints • Coordination, agility, and balance • Improving reflexes • Communication, including listening skills and problem solving
Bulldog (15 min)	Put the entire group inside a playing area of 20 × 20 to 30 × 30 yd. Two players start off as the bulldogs, wearing bibs. The two bulldogs try to work together to "hit" a player without a bib with a ball below the knees. When a player gets hit, she puts on a bib and joins the bulldogs. Play for a set time or until a single player remains.	• Passing • Thinking ahead • Receiving • Speed of play

Activity	Description	Coaching points
6v6 match (25 min)	Play a match according to US Youth Soccer U10 modified rules. The coach has a supply of balls to keep the match flowing.	• Summation of all challenges for the players (remember—stay out of their way and let them play)
Cool-down (10 min)	In a space 10 × 10 yd, players move without contact with one another for 1 min. They should move at varied speeds and in different directions—forward, sideways, and backward. They can also twirl, hop, skip, and so on. After 1 min, ask them to stop and stretch. Repeat the activity for 30 sec, and then ask your players to stop and stretch once more.	• Lowering heart rate and body temperature

US Youth Soccer

PLANS

Sample U12 Training Plan

Objective
Passing and receiving

Equipment
1 ball for each player, 2 regulation goals for the U12 age group (cones or corner flags can be used in lieu of goals), 24 cones, 4 corner flags, 14 training bibs (7 of one color and 7 of another)

Activity	Description	Coaching points
Warm-up (10 min)	Each player must kick the ball into the air, receive it, and change direction with a dribble. This is done on the coach's count. Depending on the ability of your players, the count will be short or long. You can also ask your players to dribble to the nearest line after they receive the ball.	• Encourage players to move and visually track the ball simultaneously. • Observe the execution of receiving and dribbling.
Receive and pass (15 min)	Mark off a 20 × 20 yd grid. Have spare balls with you on the side of the grid. Play a ball into the grid of four players. The players control the ball and pass it to each other so that every player touches it at least twice.	• Observe the players' touch in both passing and receiving.
Receive and pass with pressure (15 min)	Perform the same activity as above, only now after the coach plays the ball, a defending player tries to disrupt the passes. Afterward, take this same activity to the goal, using different numbers of attackers and defenders.	• See which players use the proper pass to get out of trouble. • Encourage players to shoot when the opportunity arises.
Group activity (20 min)	This activity should be played on half the field. Divide the number of players into two teams. A team must complete four, five, or six passes before shooting on goal. Each time a team loses possession, the pass count begins again.	• Look for good choices on the part of the players. See which players move without the ball (indicates thinking—when and where movement).

Activity	Description	Coaching points
Cool-down (10 min)	Have your players balance on one leg with the other leg straight in front of them. Then have them perform the following actions: 1. Pull toes back. 2. Point toes down. 3. Turn foot in. 4. Turn foot out. Next, have your players lie on their backs, bending one knee in toward the chest. Then ask them to straighten the bent leg upward. Make certain they don't use the hand to hold or pull the leg. Once the leg is extended, ask them to rotate the foot out away from the midline of the body and then in toward the midline.	• Lowering heart rate and body temperature • Loosening muscles

US Youth Soccer

PLANS

Sample U14 Training Plan

Objective
Tackling

Equipment
1 ball for each player, 2 regulation goals for the U14 age group (cones or corner flags can be used in lieu of goals), 24 cones, 4 corner flags, 16 training bibs (8 of one color and 8 of another)

Activity	Description	Coaching points
Warm-up (10 min)	Pair players up with one ball. The ball is stationary. The players in the pair stand one step away from the ball, facing each other. On your command, the players step forward simultaneously, each tackling the ball with the same foot (both with the right foot or both with the left foot). Ask your players to do 10 repetitions with each foot.	• Focus • Increasing blood flow and breathing rate
1v2 match (10 min, played in 20 sec increments)	In unrestricted space, ask your players to practice passing in groups of three. On the coach's signal, the player with the ball tries to beat the other two players in his group.	• Communication
1v1 match (10 min, played in 30 sec increments)	Mark 15 × 10 yd grids. Divide players into pairs and have them play 1v1 for 30 sec. Rest for 30 sec between bouts to emphasize coaching points. After two bouts, ask players to switch partners.	• Angle and speed of approach • Block tackling

Activity	Description	Coaching points
3v3 match (15 min)	Set up a 25 × 20 yd grid, with one goal at one end and two small goals at the other. Have players play 3v3. During the first bout of play, the third teammate acts as a support player, getting into a position to assist the other two. Afterward, the coach can provide support. All balls out of bounds are restarted from the top of the playing area. The first team to score three goals wins the bout. Play no more than two consecutive bouts per team.	• When to tackle • Choice of type of tackle • Possession or dispossession • Technique of tackle
4v4 match (15 min)	Set up a 45 × 35 yd grid with two goals. Play a match to 12 points. If a player tackles within the final third of the field, her team receives 4 points. A goal is worth 1 point.	• Committing fully to the tackle
6v6 match (20 min)	Set up a 55 × 45 yd grid with two goals. Play a match without restrictions or conditions. First team to 5 goals wins.	• Observe players' tackles and recognition of when to tackle.
Cool-down (10 min)	Inside the penalty area, players slowly jog from one side to the other and then do two stationary stretches. Reduce space to between the penalty spot and one side of the penalty area, and again players slowly jog from side to side and do two different stationary stretches. Then players move into the goal area, slowly jog from side to side, and do two different stationary stretches.	• Lowering heart rate and body temperature • Promoting team unity

US Youth Soccer

Constructing training plans requires both organization and flexibility on your part. Don't be intimidated by the amount of material you've listed in your season plan as skills and tactics you want to cover. Pick out a few basics, and build your initial training plans around them; this process will get easier after you've drafted a few plans. Then you can move from teaching simple concepts and skills to drawing up plans that introduce more complex ones. Build in some flexibility; if you find that what you've planned for the training session isn't working, have a backup activity that approaches the skill or concept from a different angle. The priorities are to keep your team playing the game and to help everyone have fun while they're learning.

As a final note, remember that the development of soccer players is a continuum and that progressive development overlaps age groups. The following should be your top 10 objectives for player development:

1. Develop each child's appreciation of the game.
2. Keep winning and losing in proper perspective.
3. Be sensitive to each child's development needs.
4. Educate players on the technical, tactical, physical, and psychological demands of the game for their level of play.
5. Implement rules and equipment modifications according to the players' age group.
6. Allow players to experience all positions.
7. Help players have fun, and provide positive feedback.
8. Conduct training in the spirit of enjoying and learning.
9. Provide the appropriate number of training sessions and matches according to the players' stage of development.
10. Strive to help all players reach their full potential and be prepared to move to the next stage of development.

Appendix

This appendix contains checklists and forms. You may reproduce and use these checklists and forms as needed for your soccer program. Please note that it is important to review all forms and checklists on an annual basis. All legal forms should be evaluated by your local legal counsel and insurance agent to properly reflect your program and relevant state and local laws.

Facilities and Equipment Checklist

Field Surface

- ❏ Sprinkler heads and openings are at grass level.
- ❏ The field is free of toxic substances (lime, fertilizer, and so on).
- ❏ The field is free of low spots or ruts.
- ❏ The playing surface is free of debris.
- ❏ No rocks or cement slabs are on the field.
- ❏ The field is free of protruding pipes, wires, and lines.
- ❏ The field is not too wet.
- ❏ The field is not too dry.
- ❏ The field lines are well marked.

Outside Playing Area

- ❏ The edge of the playing field is at least six feet from trees, walls, fences, and cars.
- ❏ Nearby buildings are protected (by fences, walls) from possible damage during play.
- ❏ Storage sheds and facilities are locked.
- ❏ The field area (ground surface and equipment) is in safe condition.
- ❏ The fences or walls lining the area are in good repair.
- ❏ Sidewalks are without cracks, separations, or raised concrete.

Equipment

- ❏ Goals are held securely together.
- ❏ Goals are secured to the ground.
- ❏ Players' equipment passes inspection, fits properly, and complies with the rules.

From American Sport Education Program, 2011, *Coaching youth soccer* (Champaign, IL: Human Kinetics).

Informed Consent Form

I hereby give my permission for _____ to participate in _____ during the soccer season beginning on _____. Further, I authorize the school or club to provide emergency treatment of any injury or illness my child may experience if qualified medical personnel consider treatment necessary and perform the treatment. This authorization is granted only if I cannot be reached after a reasonable effort to do so.

Parent or guardian: _____

Address: _____ Phone: (   )_____

Cell phone: (   )_____ Beeper number: (   )_____

Other person to contact in case of emergency: _____

Relationship to person: _____ Phone: (   )_____

Family physician: _____ Phone: (   )_____

Medical conditions (e.g., allergies, chronic illness): _____

_____

_____

_____

My child and I are aware that participating in _____ is a potentially hazardous activity. We assume all risks associated with participation in this sport, including but not limited to falls, contact with other participants, the effects of weather and traffic, and other reasonable conditions of risk associated with the sport. All such risks to my child are known and appreciated by my child and me.

We understand this informed consent form and agree to its conditions.

Child's signature: _____ Date: _____

Parent's or guardian's signature: _____ Date: _____

Adapted, by permission, from M. Flegel, 2008, *Sport first aid*, 4th ed. (Champaign, IL: Human Kinetics), 15.
From American Sport Education Program, 2011, *Coaching youth soccer* (Champaign, IL: Human Kinetics).

Injury Report Form

Date: _____ Time: _____ a.m. p.m.

Location: _____

Player's name: _____ Age: _____ Date of birth: _____

Type of injury: _____

_____

Anatomical area involved: _____

_____

Cause of injury: _____

_____

Extent of injury: _____

_____

Person administering first aid (name): _____

First aid administered: _____

_____

Other treatment administered: _____

_____

Referral action: _____

_____

Signature of person administering first aid: _____

Date: _____

Emergency Information Card

Player's name: _____ Age: _____

Address: _____

Phone: ( )_____

Provide information for parent or guardian and one additional contact in case of emergency:

Parent's or guardian's name: _____

Address: _____

Phone: ( )_____ Other phone: ( )_____

Additional contact's name: _____

Relationship to player: _____

Address: _____

Phone: ( )_____ Other phone: ( )_____

Insurance Information

Name of insurance company: _____

Policy name and number: _____

Medical Information

Physician's name: _____ Phone: ( )_____

Is your child allergic to any drugs? *YES* *NO*

If so, what? _____

Does your child have other allergies (e.g., bee stings, dust)? _____

Does your child have any of the following? *asthma* *diabetes* *epilepsy*

Is your child currently taking medication? *YES* *NO*

If so, what? _____

Does your child wear contact lenses? *YES* *NO*

Is there additional information we should
know about your child's health or
physical condition? *YES* *NO*

If yes, please explain: _____

Parent's or guardian's signature: _____ Date:_____

From American Sport Education Program, 2011, *Coaching youth soccer* (Champaign, IL: Human Kinetics).

Emergency Response Card

Be prepared to give the following information to an EMS dispatcher.

Caller's name: _____

Telephone number from which the call is being made: (____)_____

Reason for call: _____

_____

How many people are injured: _____

Condition of victim(s): _____

_____

First aid being given: _____

_____

Location: _____

Address: _____

City: _____

Directions (e.g., cross streets, landmarks, entrance access): _____

_____

Note: Do not hang up first. Let the EMS dispatcher hang up first.

From American Sport Education Program, 2011, *Coaching youth soccer* (Champaign, IL: Human Kinetics).

Glossary

assistant referee—An official who supports the head referee. Assistant referees watch the touchlines and use flags to signal the referee when various situations occur, such as a foul the referee might have missed, an offside, or an out-of-bounds ball.

ball side—The side of the field on which the ball is in play at a given time.

block tackle—An attempt to prevent an attacker from maintaining possession of the ball by blocking it with the inside of the foot while the attacker is attempting to dribble it the other way.

caution—A disciplinary action against player misconduct, initiated by the referee and signaled with a yellow card. It is officially recorded, and a second offense can cause the player to be ejected from the game (signaled by a red card).

center circle—The circle in the center of the field surrounding the kickoff spot, outside of which the defending team must remain until the ball is put into play at a kickoff.

center forward—The centermost forward, who usually leads the forwards' attack and scores most of the goals.

center mark—The spot in the center circle (also the midpoint of the halfway line) where the ball is positioned for kickoffs.

charging—Using the shoulder to bump the shoulder of an attacker in order to take away the ball (the only deliberate body contact that is legal in soccer).

corner arc—The four 1-yard arcs, one in each corner of the field of play, from which players take corner kicks.

corner kick—A direct free kick taken from a corner arc by a member of the attacking team if the ball goes out of bounds across the goal line and was last touched by a member of the defending team.

cover—A defensive concept in which a defender goes goalside to provide backup for a teammate who is challenging an attacker for possession of the ball.

defenders—Defenders play near their own team's goal and try to prevent the other team from shooting the ball. They also receive the ball from the goalkeeper and move the ball up the field to begin the attack.

direct free kick—A free kick resulting from foul play that may go directly into the goal to score, without another player having to touch the ball.

diving—A move by which the goalkeeper stops or repels shots (usually low or medium high) aimed at the goal.

dribbling—Controlling and moving the ball along the ground with light touches of the feet.

drop ball—A ball the referee drops between two opposing players to resume the game after play has been stopped (but no penalty has been called); a player may score a goal directly from a drop-ball kick. The ball is dropped at the spot where it was last in play, unless it was in the goal area. In the latter case the referee drops the ball at the nearest point outside the goal area.

ejection—Banishing a player from the field. It is a disciplinary action (signaled by a red card and put into the official record) that the referee takes against a player who has committed a personal foul or a deliberate handball.

far post—The goalpost farthest from the ball at a given time.

feinting—Using a fake move to fool an opponent.

first-touch pass—Kicking or heading the ball to pass it without first stopping it.

forwards—Forwards play closer to the other team's goal and shoot the ball more than other players. The forwards that play nearest the touchlines are called wings; those in the middle of the field are referred to as strikers.

free kick—A placekick awarded to a team when a player on the other team receives a penalty. It can be a direct kick or an indirect kick, depending on the seriousness of the opposing team's offense. Players on the offending team must stay a certain number of yards (related to the size of the center circle for the age group) away from the ball until the kicker moves it, unless they are between the goalposts of their own goal line.

fullback—A player who is part of a team's back line of defense, just in front of the goalkeeper. The primary assignment of fullbacks (also called backs) is to repel attacks on their team's goal.

goal—The area into which players try to shoot the ball to score points. A goal sits in the middle of the goal line at each end of the playing field but extends past the field itself. It is marked by two goalposts, a crossbar, and netting.

goal area—The small box immediately in front of the goal, from which players take the goal kick.

goalkeeper—A goalkeeper plays in front of the goal and tries to prevent the ball from getting into the goal. The goalkeeper is the only player allowed to use the hands to block shots and to initiate the attack from within the team's penalty area.

goal kick—A placekick that a defending player takes from the goal area when a ball that an attacking player was the last to touch goes out of bounds across the goal line. All members of the attacking team must stay outside the penalty area until the ball clears it and is back in play.

goal line—The end line of the field, on which the goal sits. The goal line runs from corner to corner.

goalside—Any position between the ball and the goal of the defending team.

halfway line—The line that runs across the field of play from touchline to touchline and divides the field in half.

handball—Intentional use of the hands on the ball by any player except the goalkeeper.

heading—Propelling and guiding the ball by striking it with the forehead, between the eyebrows and the hairline.

holding—Using the hands or arms to obstruct the movements of an opposing player, constituting a personal foul.

indirect free kick—A free kick that must be touched by a player other than the one who kicked it before it can score a goal; also refers to a particular penalty the referee calls for minor fouls.

juggling—A training technique used to develop ball control, in which a player uses any part of the body other than the hands and arms to keep the ball in the air continuously.

kickoff—A placekick that starts the game, restarts the game after a goal is scored, or starts the second half of the game. It is taken from the center spot, and players may score a goal directly from a kickoff; however, opposing players must remain outside the center circle until the ball is in play.

man-to-man defense—A defensive strategy in which each defending player is responsible for marking a specific attacking player.

marking—Defending against an opponent.

midfielders—Midfielders are all-purpose players who take shots and try to steal the ball from the other team. They are transition players, helping move the ball from defense to offense. Their position is named appropriately since they play between forwards and defenders on the field.

near post—The goalpost nearest the ball at a given time.

obstruction—When a player deliberately hinders an opponent's progress instead of playing the ball.

offside—Getting between the other team's goal line and the ball at the moment the ball is played by a teammate. The offside rule has exceptions: A player cannot be called offside if an opponent, not a teammate, last played the ball; if she received the ball directly from a corner kick, goal kick, throw-in, or drop ball; if she doesn't go closer to the opponent's goal line than at least two opponents are; or if she is in her own team's half of the field.

off the ball—Describes players who are not near the ball.

out of play—Description for a ball that has gone completely across the goal line or a touchline.

passing—Kicking or heading a ball to direct it toward a teammate.

penalty arc—An arc drawn outside the penalty area, at a radius similar to the one for the center circle, from the penalty spot. No players are allowed within this arc when a penalty kick is being taken.

penalty area—The large box in front of the goal, within which the goalkeeper may legally use hands on the ball. When the defending team commits a foul inside the penalty area that normally gives the offense a direct free kick, the foul instead results in a penalty kick.

penalty kick—A direct free kick that the referee awards to the offensive team when a member of the defensive team commits a major foul while inside his own team's penalty area. The attacker takes the kick from the penalty spot and can score a goal directly from the kick. The goalkeeper must stay on his team's goal line until the ball is kicked, but all other players must stay outside the penalty area, no closer than 10 yards from the penalty spot, until the attacker kicks the ball.

penalty mark—A location 12 yards in front of the midpoint of the goal line. Also called the penalty spot or penalty kick spot, it is the place from which players take penalty kicks.

placekick—A kick taken from a stationary position that starts or restarts the game.

punching—Hitting the ball with the fists to deflect the ball or save a goal. Only the goalkeeper may punch the ball, and only from within the penalty area.

punt—A kicking technique in which the goalkeeper drops the ball and then kicks it before it hits the ground.

receiving—The act of first collecting the ball and then getting control of it before putting it into play.

referee—The official who has overall responsibility for a match and works with two assistant referees.

restart—Any of the methods for starting up play again after it has been stopped—for example, the placekick, the throw-in, and the drop ball.

save—The goalkeeper's successful attempt to prevent a score by catching or repelling a ball headed for the goal.

shielding—Positioning oneself between the ball and an opponent while dribbling in order to keep the opponent from gaining possession of the ball.

shooting—Attempting to score by kicking the ball toward the goal.

tackling—Using the feet or charging with the shoulder to gain possession of the ball from an opponent.

throw-in—A way to get the ball back into play after it has gone out of bounds over a touchline. Standing at the point at which the ball left the field, the player (one of the opponents of the player who last touched the ball) holds the ball over her head with both hands and throws it onto the field. She must keep part of each foot on the ground, either behind or on the touchline. Players can score a goal directly from a throw-in.

touchline—The sideline that runs the length of the field of play from corner to corner.

trapping—Stopping the ball while in a stationary position.

volley kick—A kick that a player takes when the ball is still in the air.

wall—A way to help the goalkeeper defend against free kicks. At least two other defensive players line up with the keeper to form a human barrier between the kicker and the goal, but they must stand a required distance away from the ball (equal to the radius of the center circle for that age group).

wall pass—A pass in which a receiver is used to redirect the path of the ball while the passer runs to get open to receive a return pass.

weak side—The side of the field where the ball is not in play at a given time.

wingbacks—Fullbacks assigned to positions near the touchlines (also known as outside backs), who with the other defenders and goalkeeper form the line of defense closest to their own goal.

wingers—Forwards assigned to positions near the touchlines (also called outside forwards), whose responsibility is to bring the ball up the touchlines and pass into scoring range for other attacking players.

wings—The sides of the field, along the right and left touchlines.

zone defense—A defensive strategy in which defenders cover a specific area of the field rather than a specific defender; they must cover any opponent who enters their zone.

About the Authors

US Youth Soccer is the largest member of the United States Soccer Federation, with more than 3 million youth players and over 300,000 coaches. US Youth Soccer provides healthy activity through recreation and small-sided games programs that emphasize fun and de-emphasize winning at all costs.

Content expert **Sam Snow** is the director of coaching for US Youth Soccer. Snow joined the US Youth Soccer Technical Department in 2003 as the assistant director of coaching education and assumed his current role in 2004.

Snow has earned the United States Soccer Federation A license and National Youth license, a premier diploma, and a national goalkeeping coaching license. Coaching is second nature for him: He's coached at the high school (Norfolk Catholic High School), collegiate (Florida Southern College, University of South Florida, Virginia Wesleyan College), state (Florida Youth Soccer Association), and regional (US Youth Soccer Olympic Development Program Region III) levels.

Before joining the US Youth Soccer Technical Department, Snow held positions as a US Soccer national staff instructor and a director of coaching for the Louisiana Soccer Association. Snow received his bachelor's degree from Virginia Wesleyan College in 1977 and his master's degree in physical education from the University of South Florida in 1979.

The **American Sport Education Program (ASEP)**, a division of Human Kinetics, is the leading provider of youth, high school, and elite-level sport education programs in the United States. Rooted in the philosophy of "Athletes first, winning second," ASEP has educated more than 1.5 million coaches, officials, sport administrators, parents, and athletes. For 30 years, local, state, and national sport organizations have partnered with ASEP to lead the way in making sport a safe, successful, and enjoyable experience for all involved. For more information on ASEP sport education courses and resources, call 800-747-5698, e-mail ASEP@ hkusa.com, or visit www.ASEP.com.

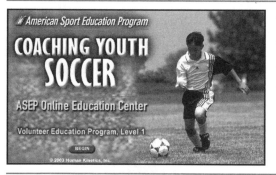

New soccer app for on-the-go youth soccer coaches

Developed by the American Sport Education Program (ASEP), **Go Coach Soccer** offers 19 video clips and 23 animations demonstrating 24 skills and 30 activities to organize your practice. Supplemental coaching tips and advice, safety guidelines and checklists, and guidance on season and practice plans will help you manage team activities beyond the Xs and Os. Go Coach Soccer will help turn chaos into productive practices and games!

Go Coach Soccer brings coaching content to your fingertips:

Skills
Attacking
Defending
Goalkeeping

Activities
Attacking
Passing
Receiving
Heading
Shooting
Defending
Goalkeeping

Advice
Practice and Season Plans
Summary of Rules
Preparing for Medical Situations
Tips for Coaching Young Athletes
Becoming a Better Coach

Square up the hips and shoulders to the receiver and turn out the kicking foot.

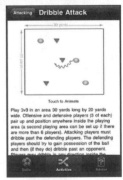

Play 3v3 in an area 30 yards long by 20 yards wide. Offensive and defensive players (3 of each) pair up and position anywhere inside the playing area (a second playing area can be set up if there are more than 6 players). Attacking players must dribble past the defending players. The defending players should try to gain possession of the ball and then (if they do) dribble past an opponent.

Download Go Coach Soccer on the Apple App Store

American Sport Education Program
A DIVISION OF HUMAN KINETICS

HUMAN KINETICS